Welcome to

2004

This edition has been researched and written
by
Anne Speight

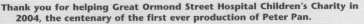

Thank you for helping Great Ormond Street Hospital Children's Charity in 2004, the centenary of the first ever production of Peter Pan.

The rights of Peter Pan were bequeathed by JM Barrie to GOSH. The value of this fantastic legacy remains a secret, at Barrie's request, in keeping with the magic and mystery of Peter Pan.

Celebrating 100 Years of Peter Pan

Through the sales of these guides we will have raised over £30,600. Since 1998 we have contributed to the funding of a mobile X-ray unit, syringe pumps, infusion pumps and a hoist, but this year we are committed to helping with a much bigger project tackling the hospital infrastructure. This 10-year redevelopment programme will upgrade the Hospital and increase its overall size enabling treatment for over 20% more patients. In the pursuit of excellence, the plan will bring the hospital right up to date with modern day medical practices and clinical care.

Funds contributed in 2004 will go towards the first stage of the re-development. A brand new Patient and Accommodation Centre, opening in 2004, will include 30 rooms for children who require short-stay treatments, along with their families. It will also contain eight transitional care flats for children who are well enough to leave their wards but need some care before they are allowed to return home.

We are proud to announce that a 6p contribution to the above charity will be made for each 'Let's Go with the Children' book sold this season. Thank you for your support. Registered charity No. 235825 ©1989 GOSHCC. 2003 GOSHCC

Getting yourself involved

Great Ormond Street Hospital Children's Charity needs everyone's support as they aim to raise over £20 million each year. There are many ways to get involved from trekking in Namibia to attending musical concerts. Log on to www.gosh.org or call 0207 916 5678 for an up to date listing of planned events, some of which can involve the whole family. Look out particularly for special Peter Pan themed events throughout the year.

Published by **Cube Publications**, 290 Lymington Road,
Highcliffe, Christchurch, Dorset BH23 5ET
Telephone: 01425 279001 Fax: 01425 279002
www.cubepublications.co.uk
Email: enquiries@cubepublications.co.uk
5th edition
ISBN 1 903594 37 5

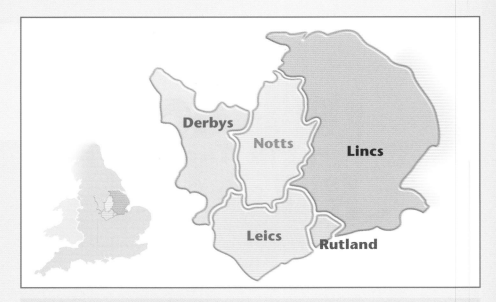

How to use this guide

This guide is one of a set of 13 covering all the counties of England and each county in this edition is colour coded as shown on the map above.

There are several chapters of subject interest as listed in the Contents opposite enabling you to choose something specific for you and your children to do or somewhere for you all to go.

If you have young children who love animals, dip into the Farms, Wildlife & Nature Parks chapter, or, if you have active teenagers, take a look at the Sports & Leisure chapter where you will find something to keep them busy.

Check out History, Art & Science and widen young horizons or choose a nearby venue from the Free Places chapter. A surprising number of things are free.

Whatever your budget, plan a day out to include a variety of activities. You may like to hire a boat, take a train ride, visit a really interesting museum, go bowling, stop off at a soft play centre, try snow sports, visit a zoo or go for a hike. Whatever interests you and your family, there is information included within the following chapters to help you occupy a wet afternoon, a long weekend or the whole school holidays.

We have highlighted price bands, facilities for school trips, places that are open all year and places that cater for birthday parties, but please call in advance if you have special needs or want particular information.

Whether you live locally or you are just visiting, you will find an amazing wealth of diverse interests, entertainments and activities in this area for children of all ages. We hope you will discover more about the area than you thought you already knew.

Please write to us with any constructive comments on the guide. We shall be delighted to hear from you. Our address is on page 1.

Use this guide with a good geographical map to help you find your way. Discover somewhere new, plan your route and keep the children busy by encouraging them to help with the navigating.

Contents

Key

Price codes are given as a maximum entry cost for a family of four, (2 Adults, 2 children):
A: £10 **B**: £20 **C**: £30 **D**: £40 **E**: £50 **F**: FREE **G**: Over £50 **P**: Pay as you go

Schools   School party facilities, visits by arrangement
Birthdays   Birthday parties are organised here
NT   National Trust property - www.nationaltrust.org.uk
EH   English Heritage property - www.english-heritage.org.uk

Telephone Numbers are provided for most entries.
Should you require special facilities for someone with a disability, please call before your visit to check suitability.

Opening Times

LAST ADMISSIONS
Many last admission times are an hour before the quoted closing time. If in any doubt, phone and ask if you know you will be arriving late. Don't get caught out and be disappointed!

WINTER AND CHRISTMAS OPENING
Many attractions close earlier in Winter and most are closed over Christmas and New Year. If you want to visit in this period, call in advance to check! At the time of going to print not all opening times were decided. We have suggested you phone for opening times if this was the case!

USEFUL INFORMATION

LOCAL COUNCILS

The Local Councils have Leisure Services Departments looking after a wide range of leisure facilities, many of which are featured within this guide, from the best parks and open spaces to sports facilities and museums. They may be able to provide further information on special events and playschemes organised for children, particularly in the school holidays.

DERBYSHIRE: Derbyshire County Council **01629 580000,** Amber Valley **01773 570222,** Bolsover **01246 240000,** Chesterfield **01246 345345,** Derby City **01332 293111,** Derbyshire Dales **01629 580580,** Erewash **0115 946 1321,** High Peak **01457 851600,** South Derbyshire **01283 221000.**

LEICESTERSHIRE: Leicestershire County Council **0116 232 3232,** Blaby **0116 275 0555,** Charnwood **01509 263151,** Harborough **01858 410000,** Hinckley and Bosworth **01455 248141,** Leicester **0116 254 9922,** Melton **01664 567771,** North West Leicestershire **01530 454545,** Oadby and Wigston **0116 288 8961.**

LINCOLNSHIRE: Lincolnshire County Council **01522 552222,** Boston Borough **01205 314200,** East Lindsey **01507 601111,** Lincoln City **01522 881188,** North Kesteven **01529 414155,** South Holland **01775 761161,** South Kesteven **01529 414155,** West Lindsey **01427 616466.**

NOTTINGHAMSHIRE: Nottinghamshire County Council **0115 982 3823,** Ashfield **01623 450000,** Bassetlaw **01909 533533,** Broxtowe **0115 917 7777,** Gedling **0115 901 3901,** Mansfield **01623 463463,** Newark and Sherwood **01636 605111,** Nottingham City **0115 915 5555,** Rushcliffe **0115 981 9911.**

RUTLAND: Rutland County Council **01572 722577.**

LEICESTERSHIRE: Charnwood www.charnwoodonline.net **01509 218113.** This is Leicestershire at its most varied with rocky summits, glorious woodland and the attractive River Soar with boating facilities at Sileby and Barrow. Much of this beautiful countryside can be accessed freely and there are suggested circular walks, wildlife events and a programme of ranger led family activities. Spend some time at Stonehurst Family Farm and get close to the animals. There are also historic buildings such as the ruins of Bradgate House, the home of Lady Jane Grey, nine days Queen of England. For something completely different visit the John Taylor Bell Foundry and see molten metal being poured. The most famous bell made there now hangs in St Paul's, London. Used extensively in film and TV drama, the Great Central Railway is spectacular with huge thunderous steam engines running every day. Young children always enjoy the Santa Specials and `Thomas' weekends. Loughborough, the main town in Charnwood, has a traditional street market, theatre, cinema, local history museum, park and leisure centre. Swimming is also available at the South Charnwood Pool or at Loughborough University where there is an Olympic-sized pool. Dip into any of the chapters in this book to find a wealth of places to visit and things to do in Leicestershire. Charnwood is easily accessed via the M1 or A6 and there are good bus and rail links. **Check out outside back cover.**

TOURIST INFORMATION CENTRES

Tourist Information Centres are a great complement to this guide. They provide details on local events such as festivals, children's workshops, guided family walks and nature discovery days. They also have local information about accommodation for visitors, as well as leaflets on many of the attractions featured in this guide.

DERBYSHIRE: Ashbourne: **01335 343666.** Bakewell: **01629 813227.** Buxton: **01298 25106.** Castleton: **01433 620679.** Chesterfield: **01246 345777.** Derby: **01332 255802.** Edale: **01433 670207.** Glossop: **01457 855920.** Matlock: **01629 583388.** Matlock Bath:

cont.on page 6

Please mention this guide when visiting attractions.

Look what you can do!

Sherwood Forest Country Park p23

Wonderland Pleasure Park p11

On Your Marques p9

SnowDome p47

USEFUL INFORMATION continued

01629 55082. Ripley: 01773 841488. Upper Derwent Valley: 01433 650953.
LEICESTERSHIRE: Ashby-de-la-Zouch: 01530 411767. Coalville: 01530 813608.
Hinkley: 01455 635106. Leicester: 0116 299 8888. Loughborough: 01509 218113.
Market Harborough: 01858 821270. Melton Mowbray: 01664 480992.
LINCOLNSHIRE: Alford: 01507 462143. Boston: 01205 356656. Brigg: 01652
657053. Cleethorpes: 01472 323111. Grantham: 01476 406166. Grimsby: 01427
615411. Horncastle: 01507 526636. Lincoln: 01522 873213 and 01522 873256. Louth:
01507 609289. Mablethorpe: 01507 474939. Scunthorpe: 01724 297354. Skegness:
01754 764821. Sleaford: 01529 414294. Spalding: 01775 725468. Stamford: 01780
755611. Sutton-on-Sea: 01507 441373. Woodhall Spa: 01526 353775.
NOTTINGHAMSHIRE: Newark: 01636 655765. Nottingham: 0115 915 5330.
Ollerton: 01623 824545. Retford: 01777 860780. West Bridgford: 0115 977 3558.
Worksop: 01909 501148.
RUTLAND: Oakham: 01572 724329. Rutland Water: 01572 653026.
LEICESTERSHIRE: Melton Mowbray: Tourist Information Centre,
www.meltononline.co.uk (e-mail: tic@melton.gov.uk) 01664 480992. For ideas of where to
visit, including Ye Olde Pork Pie Shoppe, Melton Cattle Market and the recently opened
Twinlakes Park. You will find a monthly 'What's On' factsheet, souvenirs and postcards,
together with suggested circular family walks and details of the Jubilee Way, a 15 mile
footpath that leads to Belvoir Castle. Local event ticket sales, accommodation booking,
photocopying service and a wide range of UK holiday brochures are also available.

Adventure & Fun

This chapter has lots of suggestions for both indoor and outdoor fun, from soft play centres for tiny tots to white knuckle rides for teenagers. Try a laser game, model car racing or virtual soccer. Explore a maze together, and don't forget the ever-popular water fun with wave machine and flumes. For a really special treat the region has some of the best theme parks in the country.

DERBYSHIRE

Ashbourne (near), Alton Towers, www.alton-towers.co.uk 0870 520 4060. Located on the Staffordshire border, off the B5032. Plummet vertically, whoosh upside down, experience flying, ride in the dark and get absolutely soaked. The big rides here are designed to thrill. Dare you ride them all? Don't miss 'Spinball Whizzer' the new family thrill ride. There are also gardens, pagoda fountain, live shows and special events. Open daily, 27th Mar-31st Oct. Park opens 9.30am, rides 10am. Closing times vary. Schools **Price G.**

Clay Cross, Chuckles Play Centre, Bridge Street, 01246 860049. Indoor soft play area for children under 8 years old. Climbing equipment, ball pool, bouncy castle and trikes. Separate area for under 2s. Open daily, 10am-6pm. Birthdays **Open all year** Price A.

Derby, Derby Storm, Colombo Street, www.tileisure.co.uk 01332 201768. Indoor skatepark with facilities for older children and teenagers who enjoy BMX, skateboards and blades. Open daily. Telephone for details. **Open all year.**
Freddy's Play Kingdom, 50 Nottingham Road, Spondon, 01332 662322. Indoor soft play area for under 10s, with climbing apparatus, slides and ball pools. Separate area for under 4s. Open Mon-Sat, 10am-6pm, Sun, 10am-4pm. Birthdays **Open all year** Price A.
Megazone, Willow Row Sports Centre, 01332 204004. Enjoy laser fun, plus other amusements. Open Mon-Fri, 12noon-10pm, Sat-Sun, 10am-10pm. Birthdays **Open all year** Price B.
Mundy Play Centre, Markeaton Park, 01332 343075. Outdoor play area with boating lake, climbing apparatus, bumper cars, paddling pool, crazy golf, donkey rides and land train. Some attractions are seasonal. **Open all year** Price P.
Quasar, Foresters Leisure Park, 01332 270057. Laser fun and other amusements for all the family. Open Mon-Fri, 6pm–midnight, Sat-Sun, 10am–midnight. Birthdays **Open all year** Price B.
Scally Wags, Carrington Street, 01332 294646. Indoor soft play area for under 10s and separate area for toddlers. Open daily, 9am-6.30pm. Birthdays **Open all year** Price A.
Soccerama, Ascot Drive, 01332 349193. This indoor activity centre focuses on football. Enjoy a range of virtual games and then practise at the real thing! Open daily, 12noon-8pm. Phone for price details. Birthdays **Open all year.**

Ilkeston, The American Adventure Theme Park, on A6007 signposted from M1 Jn 26, www.americanadventure.co.uk 0845 330 2929. Located around a large lake, there is something for everyone. A wide range of rides, attractions and live shows, situated in various areas such as Alamo, Fort St Lawrence and Silver City. Special events. Open daily, 3rd Apr-end Oct, from 10am, closing times vary. Schools **Price E.**
Victoria Park Leisure Centre, Manners Road, 0115 944 0400. Enjoy a fun pool with flumes, trace lights and rain storm. **Open all year.**

Langley Mill, Lanky Bill's Fun Shack, Unit 6, Cromford Road Industrial Estate, Cromford Road, 01773 767050. This newly opened soft play centre has slides, a ball pool, cargo nets, punch bags and tunnels with a separate toddlers area. Children who enjoy music, dancing and lighting effects can pop into the disco room and soft drinks are available when they need a rest! Parents can enjoy a freshly ground cappachino from the café which caters for all tastes, from ciabatta's to hot dogs. Birthday parties are held in themed party rooms. Open Mon-Thurs, 9.30am–6.30pm, (6pm in Winter), Fri-Sun, 9.30am-6pm. Birthdays **Open all year** Price A **Check out page 6.**

Longnor, **Upper Limits,** Unit 1, Buxton Road, 01298 83149. A small activity centre offering indoor climbing, indoor caving, archery and problem solving facilities. Phone for details.

Matlock Bath, **Gullivers Kingdom Theme Park,** www.gulliversfun.co.uk 01925 444888. High on the hillside are many rides and attractions designed for children under 10 yrs. Try the chair lift, log flume and lazy river boat ride. Animated and live shows. Open Easter-Oct, Sat-Sun, school hols, and most days Jun-Sept. Schools Birthdays Price C.

Matlock Bath Illuminations and Venetian Nights, 01629 55082. In a beautiful riverside setting watch a procession of uniquely created, illuminated boats. There is live music, street theatre and fun fair. Telephone TIC for dates of the cliff-top firework displays and details of park and ride facilities. Open late Aug Bank Hol–Oct, Sat-Sun evenings. Price P.

Melbourne (near), **The Ingleby Maze,** off A514, 01332 8627961. In rural countryside have fun exploring this maize maze. Quiz sheets. Phone for details. Schools Price A.

Swadlincote, **Jungle Madness,** 21 West Street, 01283 551355. Indoor play area for under 10s with ball pools, inflatable slides, bouncy castle and climbing frame. Separate area for under 5s. Open Mon-Sat, 10am-4pm, Sun, 10am-12noon. Birthdays **Open all year** Price A.

LEICESTERSHIRE

Earl Shilton, **Scalliwags,** 49 Church Street, 01455 840536. Large indoor play area for up to 14 year olds with climbing ropes, ball pool and zipline. Separate area for under 4s. Open Tues, 12noon-6pm, Wed–Fri, 10.30am-6pm, Sat-Sun, 10am-6pm, (during school hols, daily, 10am-6pm). Birthdays **Open all year** Price A.

Leicester, **Leicester Leys Leisure Centre,** Beaumont Way, 0116 233 3070. Excellent water fun in the pool with flumes and wave machine. **Open all year.**

Megazone, Belgrave Gate, 0116 253 1153. A laser game and other amusements. Open Mon-Sat, 10am-10pm, Sun, 10am-8pm. Birthdays **Open all year** Price B.

Quasar, Megabowl, St Peters Lane, 0116 251 8885. Stalk your opponents in a game of laser tag. There are other amusements and ten-pin bowling at the same centre. Open Mon-Fri from 12noon, Sat-Sun from 10am, closing times vary. Birthdays **Open all year** Price P.

Loughborough, **Street Fair,** The Market Place. Established by Royal Charter in 1221, this fair is one of the biggest street fairs in England. Many traditional rides and amusements but also lots of thrills to engage older children and teenagers. A kaleidoscope of light, sound, smell and taste. Open 11th-13th Nov. Price P.

Melton Mowbray (near), **Twin Lakes,** www.twinlakespark.co.uk 01664 567777, opened in 2003. There are lots of things to do at this centre: indoor soft play and rides, extensive outdoor play area, a variety of farm animals and boating lakes. Special events. Open daily from 10am, closing times vary. Schools Birthdays **Open all year** Price B/C.

LINCOLNSHIRE

Barton-upon-Humber (near), **Thornton Abbey Maize Maze,** Ulceby, 01469 541893. Children will love the big maze, but try starting with a quick six-minute maze. Also children's ride-on electric tractors, an adjacent 'pick-your-own' fruit farm and treasure hunt in mature woodland. Maze open mid Jul–late Sept, daily, 10am–6pm. Price B.

Boston, **Jungle Gym,** Pump Square, 01205 355244. An indoor soft play centre for children under 8 with a separate area for under 3s. Open Apr-Sept, Mon-Sat, 9.30am-4.30pm, Oct-Mar, 9.30am-6pm. Birthdays **Open all year** Price A.

Play Tower, Rochford Tower Lane, 01205 311116. An indoor activity centre with six floors of fun. Dare you ride the black hole slide? Toddlers have a separate area including ride-on cars. Telephone for details. Birthdays **Open all year.**

Bourne, Let's Play, Station Yard, South Road, 01778 425444. Indoor pirate-themed soft play centre with slides, ball pools, and 'walk the plank'. Separate toddlers' area. Open daily, 9.30am-6pm (Sun from 10am). Birthdays **Open all year** Price A.

Queens Road Leisure Centre, 01778 421435. Water fun with flume and waves. **Open all year.**

Cleethorpes, Fantasy World, Station Approach, 01472 697128. Indoor soft play area. Open Mon-Fri, 12noon–7pm, Sat-Sun and school hols, 10am-7pm. Birthdays **Open all year.**

Kingsway Leisure Centre, 01472 323200. Whatever the weather, enjoy some water fun with both a wave machine and flume. **Open all year.**

Labyrinth of Doralia, Alexandra Road, 01472 602186. Sited above an amusement arcade is this laser game. Open daily, 10.30am-9pm. Birthdays **Open all year** Price B.

Play Tower, Meridian Point, Kings Road, 01472 291300. Six floors of fun in one of the largest indoor activity centres in Britain. Enjoy the ball shooting area, slides, soft play, ball pools and climbing frames. Open Tues-Sun, Bank Hol Mons and Mons during school hols. Telephone for prices and times. Birthdays **Open all year.**

Pleasure Island, Kings Road, www.pleasure-island.co.uk 01472 211511. A family theme park with over 70 rides and attractions ranging from white knuckle rides to the Musical Time Machine, sea lion and parrot shows. Open 4th Apr–end Aug, daily, 10am-5pm (6pm Summer); Sept-Oct, Sat-Sun. Schools Price D.

Grantham, Fun Farm, Dysart Road, 01476 562228. Adjacent to the bowling alley, this indoor soft play area will provide lots of enjoyment for younger children. Open daily, 10am-6pm. Birthdays **Open all year** Price A.

Ingoldmells, Butlins, Roman Bank, 01754 765567. Day visitors are welcome to enjoy a host of attractions including traditional funfair, street theatre, waterworld, laser arena, ten-pin bowling, live shows and cinema. Open daily, Apr-Oct. Telephone for prices.

Fantasy Island, Sea Lane, www.fantasyisland.co.uk 01754 872030. A theme park with an endless array of things to do, including white knuckle rides, water rides and the SimEx Movie Ride Theatre. Open May-Oct daily, Mar-Dec, Sat-Sun, from 10am. Closing times vary. Price P.

Lincoln, Play Zone, Cross Street, 01522 539999. This indoor play centre caters for all ages. Try the drop slide, gladiator challenge, assault course or the absolute mayhem of the maze. Separate toddler area and teenagers evening! Open daily, 10am-7.15pm. Birthdays **Open all year** Price A.

Uncle Steven's, North Hykeham Sports Centre, 01522 883311. Indoor soft play with bash bags, slides and cargo net. Call for opening times. Birthdays **Open all year** Price A.

Mablethorpe, Dunes Leisure Fairground, Central Promenade, 01507 477770. Traditional fairground rides for younger children. Open daily during Summer. Price P.

Kids Adventure World, Spanish City, High Street, 01507 477310. Indoor soft play centre on three levels. Open Sat-Sun and daily in school hols, from 10.30am, closing times vary. Birthdays **Open all year** Price A.

Mumby, On Your Marques, signposted off the A52, eight miles N of Skegness www.on-your-marques.co.uk 01507 490052. This centre will fascinate model car enthusiasts, and children can have great fun with the cars on a four lane slot-car track. There are over 1,200 models in display cases offering a nostalgic journey through the world of motoring, in miniature. The displays are regularly changed so there is always something new to see and the 'Pit Stop' café sells light refreshments. Open daily, 1st Apr-31st Oct, 10am-5pm, and weekends only, Nov-Mar, 10am-4pm. **Open all year** Price A **Check out page 6.**

Visiting Relations? Going On Holiday? Gift For A Friend?

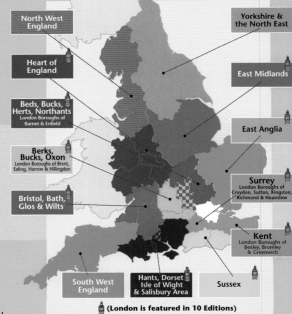

Scunthorpe, Scunthorpe Leisure Centre, 01724 280555. Enjoy the water. The pool has a wave machine and flumes. **Open all year.**

Skegness, Bottons Pleasure Beach, Grand Parade, 01754 763697. An exciting seafront fairground with a variety of rides including a white knuckle roller coaster and a pirate water ride. Something to suit everyone. Open Spring Bank Hol–Sept, daily; also Mar-Oct, school hols and weekends, 11am till late. Pay as you go or wrist band, depending on time of year.

Captain Kids Adventure World, The Pier, 01754 760600. An indoor soft play area for children up to about 10 years. Seperate toddlers' area and amusement machines. Open daily, 10am–8.30pm. **Open all year** Price A.

Laser Quest, The Pier, 01754 765858, is adjacent to the bowling alley. Space age fun on the pier! Open during school hols, daily, 10am-10pm, otherwise Mon-Fri, 5-10pm, Sat-Sun, 10am-10pm. Birthdays **Open all year** Price B.

Panda's Palace, Tower Esplanade, 01754 765494. Large, indoor soft play area for children up to about 12 years old. A super facility for when it's wet or gets too cold for the beach. Open daily, Easter-Sept and all school hols, 9.45am-6pm, otherwise Sat-Sun, 10.15am-5pm. Birthdays **Open all year** Price A.

Spalding, Fun Farm, Weston, 01406 373444. Adjacent to a large garden centre, this indoor soft play centre for under 12s includes a spooky cave, slides, and biff bash. Separate toddlers' area. Open daily, 10am–6pm. Birthdays **Open all year** Price A.

Laser Storm, Weston, 01406 373111. Opened in 2003, this centre is alongside the Fun Farm. Enjoy a laser game and other facilities such as air hockey, pool and dance machines. Open Thurs-Fri, 4-10.30pm, Sat–Sun, 1-10.30pm (school hols open daily, 1-10.30pm). Birthdays **Open all year** Price B.

Stamford, Rascals, West Sreet, 01780 480610. A soft play area on two levels for under 10 year olds. Separate area for toddlers. Open Mon-Sat, 10am–5.30pm, Sun, 10.30am-4.30pm. Birthdays **Open all year** Price A.

Stamford Leisure Centre, Drift Road, 01780 765522. Water fun with wave machine and flume. **Open all year.**

Wragby, The Wragby Maze, signposted off B1202, www.amazing-conifers.com 01673 858660. Enjoy the giant conifer maze and other outdoor attractions including putting, croquet, garden draughts and boules. Open daily, Easter–Oct, 10am-5pm. Schools Birthdays Price B.

NOTTINGHAMSHIRE

Edwinstowe (near), Sherwood Forest Fun Park, 01623 823536. Adjacent to the forest and village cricket ground, this small static fairground has dodgems, slippery slide and other amusements. Open daily, Mar-Oct, 10am-dusk, weather permitting. Price P.

Farnsfield, Wonderland Pleasure Park, White Post Island, www.wonderlandplea-surepark.com 01623 882773, is one of the largest open play areas in the region, and offers a whole host of attractions. Set in 30 acres of grounds, try a game of pitch and putt, the bumpy slide, watersplash or a ride on the miniature railway. Amongst other things, have a go on the trampolines, junior roller coaster, maze and huge adventure playground. If the weather turns overcast you can visit the cafe, or see beautiful butterflies in the giant Tropical House. Children will enjoy the indoor bouncy castle and soft play area. Although some attractions are seasonal the park is open daily, Feb-Dec, 10am-5pm, and Jan, Sat-Sun. Schools Birthdays **Open all year** Price B **Check out inside back cover.**

Long Eaton, Action Tots, Gibb Street, 0115 946 9600. Indoor soft play centre for under 9s. Open Mon-Sat, 10am-6pm, Sun, 12noon-4pm. Birthdays **Open all year** Price A.

Mansfield, Playland, Botany Avenue, 01623 654712. Indoor area for under 10s with soft play, ball pools, slides, bouncy castles and sand pit. Open daily, 10am-5pm. Birthdays **Open all year** Price A.

Water Meadows, Tichfield Park, Bath Street, 01623 463880. Enjoy the water at this fun centre with wave machine, flume, geysers, wild water rapids and beach area. Birthdays **Open all year.**

Nottingham, Goose Fair, Forest Recreation Ground, www.nottinghamgoosefair.co.uk 0115 915 6970. Europe's largest travelling fair visits to provide entertainment for all ages. All the usual amusements and some really exciting rides. Open 6th-9th Oct. Price P.

Hoods Hide Out, Beach Dale Swimming Centre, Bilborough, 0115 915 1575. Soft play area for under 10s. Open Mon and Fri, 10am-5pm. Birthdays **Open all year** Price A.

Megazone, Cranbrook Street, 0115 958 9178. Laser fun and other amusements. Open Mon-Fri, 11am-9pm, Sat, 9am-9pm, Sun, 10am-8pm. Birthdays **Open all year** Price B.

Run Riot, Rushcliffe Arena, West Bridgford, 0115 981 4027. Indoor play area on three levels with soft play and big slide. Open daily, 10am-7pm. Birthdays **Open all year** Price A.

Tumble Town, 107 High Street, Arnold, 0115 967 1161. Indoor soft play area for under 8s. Some structured play sessions are offered mid-week. Open Mon-Fri, 10am-6.30pm, Sat-Sun, 5pm. Birthdays **Open all year** Price A.

Ollerton (near), Thoresby Maze, off the A614, www.thoresby.com 01623 822216. Located in the beautiful surroundings of Thoresby Park, this new maize maze will prove to be great fun for children of all ages. Open mid Jul-mid Sept. Phone for details. Price B.

Rampton (near), Sundown Adventure Land, www.sundownadventureland.co.uk 01777 248274. A theme park designed for the very young. The attractions and rides are all connected with various nursery rhymes. Special events including visits from Santa. Telephone for opening times and prices. Schools Birthdays **Open all year.**

Free Places

This chapter includes open spaces such as beaches, moorland, waterways, woodland and farming country. There is also a selection of parks, museums and other places that offer family enjoyment, interest and entertainment for free.

Although free admission, there may be some car parking charges, extra charges for schools and special activities, or requests for donations.

DERBYSHIRE

Derbyshire is a haven for walkers and cyclists. Tourist Information Centres have details of many trails including:

Derwent Valley Heritage Way. Created in 2003, this long-distance trail links the splendour of the Upper Derwent reservoirs with the Derwent Valley Mills World Heritage Site.

Five Pits Trail. Between Grassmoor and Tibshelf. Seven miles along a former railway line, linking old colliery sites. Numerous access points. Walkers and cyclists can now enjoy rolling scenery and abundant wildlife.

High Peak Trail, 01629 823204. Scenic route for walkers and cyclists along 17 miles of former railway line between Cromford and Buxton. Links numerous sites and visitor centres. Schools.

Longdendale Trail. A walkers' and cyclists' route along former railway line between Hadfield and Woodhead tunnels. Pass by five reservoirs; watch sailing and spot wildlife in the rugged moorland.

Manifold Trail, 01298 84679. This follows the old railway line from Waterhouses to Hulme End. Various access points. Excellent for walks and cycling, beautiful valley scenery. Climb up to Thor's Cave and paddle in the river at Wetton Mill.

Monsal Trail. Eight miles along old railway line from Bakewell towards Buxton. Various access points. Some sections for cycles. Cross the famous Monsal Head viaduct. Look out for Litton Mill, a former cotton mill notorious for harsh treatment of child labourers.

Pennine Way. Famous as the first long-distance walking path. It climbs north from Edale across high moors and wild scenery.

Sett Valley Trail, 01663 746222. A walkers' and cyclists' route along three miles of the former railway line between Hayfield and New Mills. Ranger-led family activities.

Tissington Trail. A 13-mile route following the old railway line between Ashbourne and Parsley Hay. Various access points. Walking and cycling with glorious views across limestone country where wildlife abounds.

Alderwasley (near), Shining Cliff Woods, off the A6. Beautiful ancient woodland with numerous access points. In the 1700s a charcoal burner lived here, cradling her babies in one of the trees. Thought to be associated with origins of the nursery rhyme 'Rock-a-bye-baby'. **Open all year.**

Bakewell, Tea Shop Trail. The Bakewell Tart is properly called a pudding. Numerous tea-shops claim to hold the authentic recipe. Which display provides the best evidence? You will need to sample the taste! **Open all year.**

Bakewell (near), Chatsworth Parkland. Walk amongst the sheep in beautiful parkland. Admire the house from the River Derwent. Cafe/shops in Stable Courtyard. Check out 'History' and 'Farms' chapters. **Open all year.**

Bamford (near), Upper Derwent Reservoirs, 01433 650953, with access from the A57 or A6013. See three massive dams which the Dambuster squadron of the RAF used for practice raids. Spectacular scenery for walks and cycling. A ramblers' minibus operates all year on Sun and Bank Hol Mons, also Summer Sats. Picnic areas, information centre and ranger-led activities. Schools **Open all year.**

Birchover (near), Stanton Moor. With various access points this has been an important site since the Bronze Ages. Look out for old burrows, the Nine Ladies Stone Circle, a tower and the Cork Stone (a weathered pinnacle with steps cut into it). **Open all year.**

Buxton, Buxton Country Park and Grin Low. Over 100 acres of woods and high rolling grass land. Climb the folly known locally as 'Solomon's Temple'. The tower gives magnificent views. **Open all year.**

Buxton Museum and Art Gallery, Terrace Road, 01298 24658. Discover the geology, archaeology and history of the Peak District through a 'time tunnel', complete with sounds and smells of the past! Open Tues-Sat, 9.30am-5.30pm (5pm Sat), Summer Suns and Bank Hol Mons, 10.30am-5pm. Schools **Open all year.**

Pavilion Gardens, adjacent to the Opera House, has lakes, a playground, crazy golf, miniature train and hothouse with tropical plants. Sometimes there is music from the bandstand. Occasional horse and carriage rides. **Open all year.**

Town Trail, 01298 35106. A spa town since Roman times. Fill your container with water from St Ann's Well and see the Pump Room, Thermal Baths and Crescent. Good areas to play include The Slopes, Pavilion Gardens and Serpentine Walks. Contact TIC for information leaflet. **Open all year.**

Buxton (near), Goyt Valley. With exceptional scenery including the Errwood Reservoir, woodland nature trail and extensive moorland. Various picnic sites. **Open all year.**

Castleton, Mam Tor, NT. Magnificent hillside with Iron Age fort. Great place to picnic, superb views and sometimes hang-gliding to watch. Known as the 'Shivering Mountain' - notice how the old road has broken away. Winnats Pass, Lose Hill and Cave Dale are all famous beauty spots nearby. **Open all year.**

Chesterfield, Chesterfield Canal, www.chesterfield-canal-trust.org.uk 01246 274077. Good for walks and wildlife, some sections are navigable with activity at locks. Ranger-led activities and boat trips from the visitors centre at Tapton Lock. Schools **Open all year.**

Chesterfield Museum and Art Gallery, St Mary's Gate, 01246 345727. In this local history museum find out why the church has a crooked spire and watch an old video of the town. Open Thurs-Sat, Mon-Tues, 10am-4pm. Schools **Open all year.**

Queens Park. This attractive park, centrally located, has a boating lake, miniature train, playground, bandstand, cricket and wildfowl. **Open all year.**

Chesterfield (near), Linacre Reservoirs, off B6050 Cuthorpe, 01246 5670493. These small reservoirs are in an attractive wooded valley. Sit and picnic or explore the waymarked nature trails. Ranger-led activities. Schools **Open all year.**

Crich (near), Memorial Tower, 01773 852350. This local landmark, sometimes referred to as Crich Stand, is situated high on a hill. The tower was built in memory of soldiers who died in war. Climb the 58 steps for extensive views. Picnic area. Open Thurs-Tues, 9am-5pm (4pm Oct-Apr). Schools **Open all year.**

Cromford, Cromford Canal, 01629 55082. Excellent for a relaxing walk or follow a leaflet to learn about the wildlife and industrial history. Telephone the TIC for dates when the beam engine at Leawood Pumphouse is in steam. It was built to pump water from River Derwent into the canal. Schools **Open all year.**

Cromford Mill, 01629 824297. Designed by Sir Richard Arkwright, the world's first successful water-powered cotton spinning mill is now recognised as a World Heritage Site. Walk around the courtyard where display boards explain history and technology. Shops and tearoom. Special events and guided tours (small charge). Open daily, 9am-5pm. Schools **Open all year.**

Junction Workshops, Cromford and High Peak Railway (disused), 01629 822831. Original buildings and a model of how the site would have looked and videos of the old steam trains. Follow an audio tour to explore outside. Ranger-led activities. Open daily, Easter-Oct, 10.30am-5.30pm (4.30pm Oct); Nov-Easter, Sat-Sun, 10.30am-4pm. Schools **Open all year.**

Derby, Allestree Park, off Duffield Road. Scenic parkland, grounds of a former hall. Includes golf course, woodlands, a large lake with geese and nature trail. **Open all year.**

> **Derby Museums** are all open Mon, 11am-5pm, Tues-Sat, 10am-5pm, Sun and Bank Hol Mons, 2-5pm. Schools **Open all year.**
>
> **Industrial Museum,** The Silk Mill, Full Street, 01332 255308. Good displays include railway engineering since 1839 and a major collection of Rolls Royce aero engines.
>
> **Museum and Art Gallery,** The Strand, 01332 716659. Huge range of items, from Derby porcelain and local regimental history to wildlife and Egyptian mummies. Children's workshops.
>
> **Pickfords House Museum,** 41 Friar Gate, 01332 255363. Social history and costume galleries in Grade I listed building. The toilets for public use are from different eras! Special events.

Markeaton Park, off A52/A38 junction, 01332 384494. Extensive park with pitch and putt, putting, tennis, cricket, boating lake, light railway and the Mundy Play Centre. **Open all year.**

Derby (near), Elvaston Castle Country Park, 01332 571342. Grounds of former hall include lake, woods, playground, walled gardens and estate church. Park open daily, dawn-dusk. **Open all year.**

Edale, Kinder Scout, NT. Famous as scene of mass trespass in 1932. A challenging climb, past waterfalls to extensive peat bog of the summit. At 636m, the highest point in the Peak District. Fantastic views and interesting geology. **Open all year.**

Eyam, Eyam Village. An attractive place with a famous history concerning the plague of 1665. Visit the church which has lots of displays. Walk to a nearby field to see the Riley Graves (NT) where a Mrs Hancock dragged several bodies to be buried. Check out Eyam Museum in 'History' chapter. **Open all year.**

Glossop, Manor Park. Enjoy 60 acres of parkland, once the grounds of Glossop Hall. Attractive lake, crazy golf, children's playground, miniature train and tennis. Don't forget bread to feed the ducks. **Open all year.**

Great Hucklow, Camphill Farm, 01298 871270. A popular gliding centre with a spectators' area for watching take-offs and landings. Picnic and enjoy the attractive countryside. As weather dependent, telephone first. Open daily, dawn-dusk. **Open all year.**

Hartington (near), Biggin Dale, NT. Access by foot from Dale End hamlet. A nature reserve and wide grassy area for picnics. Further into the steep-sided dale, go fossil hunting in the mounds of scree. Other attractive places nearby include Beresford Dale and Wolfscote Dale. **Open all year.**

Hathersage, Church of St Michael and All Angels, 01433 650215. Find the grave of 'Little John', friend of Robin Hood. Good children's village guide explains links with Charlotte Bronte. Eyre family brasses can be rubbed. Please pay for materials used. Open daily, dawn-dusk. **Open all year.**

Hathersage (near), Stanage Edge. Picnic and watch climbers tackle the impressive crags or enjoy a walk across high moorland. Site of Special Scientific Interest. Spectacular views. Nearby Frogett Edge and Curbar Edge offer similar attractions. **Open all year.**

Heanor, Shipley Country Park, signposted off the A608, 01773 719961. Meadows, woodlands and lakes, extending to 600 acres with lots of opportunities for day ticket fishing, kite flying and cycling. Children are invited to a wildlife WATCH group which meets on a regular basis. Look out for the toddler play area, adventure playground and wooden sculpture trail. There is a full events programme with something of interest for everyone. The Visitor Centre with shop and cafe is open daily, 11am-3.30pm. Schools **Open all year** Check out page 12.

Ilam, Ilam Country Park, NT, 01335 350245. The area has lovely walks and picnic areas alongside the River Derwent. Phone for details of when the visitor centre, with exhibition panels, shop and tearoom, is open. **Open all year.**

Ilam (near), Dovedale, NT. Attractive wooded riverside. Relax and picnic by the stepping stones. Children can paddle or have a walk and see the remarkable geological formations, including Dove Holes, Jacobs Ladder, Lovers Leap and The Twelve Apostles. For the energetic, climb Thorpe Cloud. **Open all year.**

Ilkeston, Erewash Museum, High Street, 0115 907 1141. This local history museum is located in a Georgian house set on the hillside with views over the Erewash Valley. Watch out for special events with demonstrations and a chance to have a go. Open Feb-Dec, Tues, Thurs-Sat, 10am-4pm. Schools.

Matlock, Hall Leys Park. Attractive town park with gardens, children's playground, putting, tennis, miniature train, paddling pool and boating lake. **Open all year.**

Matlock Bath, Town Trail, 01629 55082. Enjoy a woodland and riverside walk with playgrounds and views to High Tor. Watch rock climbing and discover the history of the village based on its thermal waters and fine scenery. Leaflets available from TIC. **Open all year.**
Whistlestop Countryside Centre, Old Railway Station, 01629 580958. Derbyshire Wildlife Trust Information Centre with details of over 40 nature reserves, guided walks and family fun events. Open daily, Apr-Oct, 10am-5pm, Nov-Mar, Sat-Sun, 12noon-4pm. Schools **Open all year.**

Melbourne (near), Foremark Reservoir, off the A514. Alongside the reservoir there are waymarked paths, a nature reserve and play areas. Details of sailing and fishing from the information kiosk. **Open all year.**
Staunton Harold Estate, 01530 411767. Attractive location for walks by a small lake with ducks. Visit the Ferrers Craft Centre, Garden Centre and see the church (NT) which was one of the few to be built during the period of Oliver Cromwell. Tearoom. Opening times vary, telephone the TIC for details. **Open all year.**
Staunton Harold Reservoir, 01332 865081. At the northern end there is a picnic site, adventure playground, and exhibition room. Enjoy a walk and watch the sailing. Ranger-led activities. Schools **Open all year.**

Middleton (near), Middleton Top Engine House, 01629 823204. This huge restored winding engine was used to haul rail wagons up the Middleton incline on the Cromford and High Peak Raiway. Telephone for dates of guided tours when engine can be seen in steam (small charge). Schools **Open all year.**

Minninglow, Roystone Grange Trail. Take a guide book to explore this four-mile archaeological trail including a Bronze Age barrow, remains of a Roman manor house and field system, and 19th century railway, quarries and lime-kilns. **Open all year.**

Monyash, Lathkill Dale. Access on foot. This is a sheltered National Nature Reserve. Find the cave where water comes out of the ground (seasonal). Lower section of dale with attractive river, access from Over Haddon or Cocksbury Bridge. **Open all year.**

Nether Padley (near), Longshaw Estate, NT, signposted from A625, 01433 631708. There are 1,700 acres of moors, ancient woodlands and farms. Sheep dog trials every Sept. A small visitors centre with cafe is open daily, Easter-Oct, 10.30am-5pm; Winter, Sat-Sun, 10.30am-dusk. Schools **Open all year.**

New Mills, New Mills Heritage Centre, 01663 746904. Listen to the story of the five mills and see a model of the town as it was in 1884. Outside, follow an industrial heritage trail through the spectacular gorge or follow the impressive Millennium Walkway which clings to the cliff sides. Centre open Tues-Fri, 11am-4pm, Sat-Sun and Bank Hol Mons, 10.30am-4.30pm (4pm Winter). Schools **Open all year.**

Peak Forest (near), **Freshfields Donkey Village**, turn off A623 towards Wormhill, 01298 79775. Lots of different donkeys to see in field and barns. Attractive tea garden (Apr-Oct). Donations are invited for the Michael Elliott Trust which provides visits to the donkeys for children with special needs. Open daily, 10am-4pm (5pm Sat-Sun). Schools **Open all year.**

Rosliston, Rosliston Forestry Centre, Burton Road, Rosliston, www.south-derbys.gov.uk/rosliston 01283 515524 or 563483. Enjoy a quiet walk in this National Forest site following waymarked paths through young trees planted in 1993. To extend your visit make use of the Visitor Centre facilities which include soft play, adventure play, crazy golf, fishing, cycle hire, restaurant and craft shops. There are special events and school visits all year, guided tours and Bird of Prey demonstrations are available to pre-booked groups. Site open daily, 8am-dusk. Separate times for restaurant and craft shops. Schools Birthdays **Open all year.**

Staveley (near), Barrow Hill Railway Centre, 01246 854921. A fully operational roundhouse engine shed, a unique example of 19th century railway architecture. Watch restoration work on steam and diesel locomotives. Open Sat-Sun, 10am-4pm. Special events including Santa visits (charge). **Open all year.**

Wirksworth (near), Carsington Water, 01629 540696. Britain's newest reservoir is signposted off B5035. Enjoy the adventure playground, cycle hire, wildlife and bird hides, fishing and water sports. A visitors centre is open daily from 10am and there are ranger-led activities. Schools Birthdays **Open all year.**

Youlgrave (near), Bradford Dale. Children can paddle in the river and walk up the dale to look out for weirs and fish pools. Can you spot any trout? Woodlands and old mine workings. **Open all year.**

LEICESTERSHIRE

Cadeby, **The Cadeby Experience,** signposted off the A447, 01455 290462. In the old rectory garden ride on the steam-operated narrow-gauge railway. See the Boston Collection of railway artefacts and models. Also brass rubbing in church. Telephone for opening times and special events.

Castle Donington, **East Midlands Aeropark,** 01332 852852. Climbing apparatus adjacent to the runway with good views of the aeroplanes as they take off and land. Picnic area and a static collection of historic aircraft. Open Thurs and Sun, 10.30am-5pm; also Sat, Apr-Oct, 12noon-5pm. **Open all year.**

Cropston, **Cropston Reservoir Visitors Centre,** 0116 235 2014. Pre-booked groups only can take a fascinating tour of the Victorian water treatment works and old pump house. Also fieldwork opportunities around the reservoir. Schools **Open all year.**

Donington-le-Heath, **The Manor House,** 01530 831259. Restored medieval house with herb garden and tearoom. Special events include period re-enactments. Open daily, Apr-Nov, 11.30am-5pm (3pm Oct–Nov); Dec-Feb, Sat-Sun, 11.30am-3pm; Mar, daily, 11.30am-3pm. Schools **Open all year.**

Hallaton, **Hallaton Village,** signposted off A47, 01858 555416. Surrounded by glorious rolling countryside, this is a picturesque village with duck pond. Visit on Easter Bank Hol Mons to experience the ancient custom of 'Hare Pie Scrambling and Bottle Kicking' or find out about it in the local museum which is open May-Oct, Sat-Sun and Bank Hol Mons, 2.30-5pm.

Hinckley (near), **Burbage Common and Woods,** 01455 633712. There are 220 acres of ancient woodland and open pasture with access from either B4667 or off B4668, by the visitors centre and small children's playground. Ranger-led activities. Schools **Open all year.**

Ibstock, Sense Valley Forest Park, Ravenstone Road. Reclaimed colliery site, now part of the National Forest with a lot of new tree planting. There are 150 acres with three lakes, river and woodland, bird hides and fishing. **Open all year.**

Leicester, Abbey Park, Abbey Park Road. Alongside the River Soar, includes a boating lake, miniature railway, extensive pets corner, play area, floodlit synthetic pitch and tennis courts. **Open all year.**

Castle Park. Signposted from the outskirts, this is the oldest part of the city with several free museums, the Cathedral, castle mound and riverside gardens. Special events include period re-enactment. **Open all year.**

Eco House, Western Park, Hinkley Road, www.environ.org.uk 0116 254 5489. A 'show home' with displays, artefacts and video. An audio guide explores green issues on both a global and local scale. Open Wed-Fri, 2-5pm, Sat-Sun, 10am-5pm. Schools **Open all year.**

Gas Museum, Aylestone Road, www.gasmuseum.co.uk 0116 250 3190. Extensive displays recall the history of gas as a source of energy. What gas appliances can you spot? Open Tues-Thurs, 12noon-4.30pm. Schools **Open all year.**

Leicester City Museums, www.leicestermuseums.ac.uk 0116 225 4900. Summer holiday activities and special events. Open Apr-Sept, Mon-Sat, 10am-5pm, Sun, 1-5pm; Oct-Mar, Mon-Fri, 10am-4pm, Sun, 1-4pm. Schools **Open all year.**

> **Abbey Pumping Station,** adjacent to National Space Centre, 0116 299 5111. Built as part of the Victorian sewage system, it is now a Museum of Technology, with hands-on activities. On certain days there is a working narrow-gauge railway and the original giant beam engines are in steam, (small charge).
>
> **Belgrave Hall,** Church Road, 0116 266 6590. This is a small Queen Anne house with garden. Look for the nursery with three life-size models.
>
> **Guildhall,** Guildhall Lane, 0116 253 2569, is within the Castle Park area. This 14th century building includes one of the oldest town libraries in the country, also 19th century police cells.
>
> **Jewry Wall Museum,** St Nicholas Circle, 0116 225 4971. Within the Castle Park area, adjacent to the ruins of a massive Roman wall, this modern building contains archaeological finds, including floor mosaics.
>
> **New Walk Museum,** 0116 225 4900. All kinds of collections can be seen here including a dinosaur skeleton and an Ancient Egypt gallery with mummies. Special exhibitions and events.
>
> **Newarke Houses Museum,** The Newarke, 0116 225 4980, within the Castle Park area. The museum contains clocks, toys and a period street scene. The 19th century giant, Daniel Lambert, is also featured. He was huge!

Multi-Cultural Leicester, 0116 299 8888. For details of how to experience the city's mosaic of cultures contact the TIC. Asian shops along the Golden Mile, various carnivals and a variety of worship centres all offer a tantalising glimpse. The display of Diwali lights is said to be the biggest outside India. Schools.

Riverside Way. An off-road cycle route alongside the River Soar and Grand Union Canal. It links Watermead Country Park, Abbey Pumping Station, National Space Centre with Abbey Park, the Straight Mile and extending south to Aylestone Meadows. **Open all year.**

University Botanic Gardens, Stoughton Drive South, 0116 271 2933. A quiet 16-acre oasis with lots of paths to explore, beautiful trees, flowers and exotic cacti in various greenhouses. Open daily, 10am-4pm. Schools **Open all year.**

Loughborough, Charnwood Museum and Queens Park, Granby Street, 01509 233754. An award-winning local history museum with many interactive displays. Special events include children's workshops. The park has a café, aviaries, small lake and the Carillon Tower. Park open daily, dawn-dusk. Museum, Mon-Sat, 10am-4.30pm, Sun, 2-5pm. Schools **Open all year.**

Loughborough (near), Beacon Hill Country Park, 01509 890048. Covers over 300 acres with woodland, heath, rocky outcrops and farmland. Use the toposcope to identify features in the extensive views. Iron Age objects found here are on display in the Jewry Wall Museum in Leicester. Schools **Open all year.**

Broombriggs Farm and Windmill Hill, Woodhouse Eaves. A trail around this Charnwood farm has numerous information boards. On the adjacent hill find the ruins of an old windmill. Schools **Open all year.**

Outwoods and Jubilee Wood. Within Charnwood enjoy 126 acres of mixed woodland. There are many footpaths, rocky outcrops and a mass of bluebells in Spring. **Open all year.**

Market Bosworth, Market Bosworth Country Park, off the B585. This park was originally part of a larger deer park. The 87 acres have fine mature trees, lake and stream with small ponds, an arboretum, children's play area and fishing. **Open all year.**

Market Bosworth (near), Battle Trails, Bosworth Battlefield, 01455 290429. Explore well-surfaced paths through fields and woodland. There are numerous information boards. Footpaths link four access car park/picnic areas. Check out 'History' chapter. Schools **Open all year.**

Market Harborough, Harborough Museum, Adam and Eve Street, 01858 821085. An old corsetry factory, this local history museum is an Aladdin's cave. Open Mon-Sat, 10am-4.30pm, Sun, 2-5pm. Schools **Open all year.**

Melton Mowbray, Carnegie Museum, Thorpe End, 01664 569946. Local history displays concerning fox hunting, pork pies and cheese. Suitable for school visits or look out for special holiday activities. Open daily, 10am-4.30pm. Schools **Open all year.**

Melton Mowbray Country Park, off Wymondham Way, 01664 480164. Open space around a dammed lake suitable for walks or cycling. Sports pitches, small visitors centre and children's playground. Schools **Open all year.**

Melton Mowbray (near), Borough on the Hill Country Park, covers 82 acres of hilly ground crowned by an impressive Iron Age fort with well preserved ramparts. Good for kite flying and picnics. What can you see using the topograph? **Open all year.**

Mountsorrel, Mountsorrel Quarry, 0116 230 3881. One of the largest man-made holes in Europe! Rock is still being extracted from the site. Pre-booked school visits only. Schools **Open all year.**

Newton Linford, Bradgate Park, 0116 236 2713, covers 850 acres of countryside. Paddle in the stream, climb up to the folly `Old John', watch the large herd of deer and see birdlife on Cropston Reservoir. Phone for dates when the information point, Bradgate House ruins and the Deer Barn Visitors Centre (small charge) are open. Schools **Open all year.**

Oadby, Brooks Hill Environment Centre, Wigston Road, 0116 271 4514. Look out for special events and ranger-led activities at this centre which demonstrates solutions to global environmental issues. Exhibition room (small charge). Centre open Mon-Fri, 10am-5pm, Sat-Sun and Bank Hol Mons, 4pm. Schools **Open all year.**

Shacklestone, Ashby Canal. The towpath is particularly attractive between Shacklestone and Stoke Golding. It has good access points and picnic areas. Designated as a conservation area, look out for kingfishers, herons and water voles. For boat trips check out 'Trips' chapter. **Open all year.**

Sharnford (near), Fosse Meadows, signposted from B4114. Display panels around 140 acres of traditional meadows and new woodland. Home to insects, butterflies and birds. Picnic area. **Open all year.**

Swannington, Swannington Heritage Trail and Hough Mill, www.swannington-heritage.co.uk 01530 222330. Learn about ancient colliery sites and see a railway incline, engineered by Robert Stephenson. Visit the renovated mill which includes interactive exhibits. Trail leaflet and pre-booked guided tours. Mill open Apr-Sept, Suns, 2-5pm. Schools **Open all year.**

Swithland, **Swithland Woods** are 146 acres of beautiful ancient woodland for nature study, walks and picnics. Hidden in the trees are two deep water-filled quarries, well-fenced. Try and find other signs of the famous slate workings. **Open all year.**

Syston, **Watermead Country Park,** 0116 267 1944, situated on the Charnwood/Leicester City border. This area of wetland, adjacent to the River Soar and Grand Union Canal, is good for walks and cycling. Lakes, nature reserve and bird hides. Discover the local connection with King Lear and locate the Millennium Mammoth. Opportunities for fishing, watersports and ranger-led activities. Schools **Open all year.**

Thornton, **Thornton Reservoir,** 2 miles from M1 Jn 22, 01332 865081. Enjoy a walk or cycle just over a mile around the reservoir. Watch wildlife and find wooden sculptures in the wood. Day tickets for bank or boat fishing. Ranger-led activities. **Open all year.**

Worthington, **Cloud Trail,** extends to Derby Riverside Gardens. This is a super off-road cycle route following an old railway track. It passes near the famous Breeden-on-the-Hill church and crosses the River Trent near Swarkestone. **Open all year.**

Wymondham, **Wymondham Windmill**, Butt Lane, 01572 787304. Situated high in the attractive Wolds countryside, this mill is being renovated and preserved. Explore the different floors and climb to the top. Tearoom, craft units and play area. Open Easter-Oct half term, Tues-Sun, 10am-5pm; Nov-Mar, Sat-Sun, 11am-4pm. **Open all year.**

LINCOLNSHIRE

Lincolnshire has long beaches to enjoy and much open countryside:
Beaches. With sand stretching as far as the eye can see, the coast is famously bracing. Enjoy the traditional delight of bucket and spade, donkeys and ice cream. Cleethorpes, Skegness and Mablethorpe are lively with lots of amusements. Chapel St Leonards and Sutton-on-Sea are quieter.
The Fens. The area around Spalding, Boston, and Long Sutton is flat, having been drained many centuries ago. Famous for its fields of daffodils and tulips, it's possible to fish in the various rivers and drains. Combine this with a day cycling on quiet country lanes. Suggested routes include a search for King John's jewels.

Barton-upon-Humber, Baysgarth House Museum, Caistor Road, 01652 632318. Set in 30 acres of parkland, this local history museum has fine period rooms, craftsmen's displays, hands-on activities and special events. Museum open, Tues-Sun and Bank Hol Mons, 10am-4pm. Park open, dawn-dusk. Schools **Open all year.**
Far Ings Nature Reserve, Far Ings Road, 01652 634507. Run by Lincolnshire Wildlife Trust, this 100-acre site is located alongside the River Humber. Enjoy a walk and spot wildlife from the hides. A visitors centre is open Summer weekends, Bank Hols and all year on Sun afternoons. Special events. Schools **Open all year.**
Humber Bridge Viewing Area, Far Ings Road. A good spot for family relaxation, with children's play facilities. Try the exhilarating cycle ride over the bridge, or picnic and amble along the riverside. **Open all year.**
Water Edge Country Park, Maltkiln Road, 01724 297370. This newly developing country park has 86 acres with lakes, picnic areas and bird hides. Good views of the Humber Bridge. Also art gallery and heritage displays in the former ropewalk building. Special events. Schools **Open all year.**

Barton-upon-Humber (near), Thornton Abbey, Ulceby, EH. Explore the ruins of an impressive 14th century gatehouse. Picnic and enjoy a walk in the grounds. Nearby are a 'pick your own' fruit farm and maize maze. Abbey grounds open daily; Gatehouse open 1st and 3rd Sun in the month, (Winter, 3rd Sun only), 12noon-4pm.

Boston, St Botolph's Church, 01205 354670. This is the largest parish church in Europe. Climb 290 steps up the tower (small charge) and find out why it's known as 'The Stump'. Discover the link with Boston, Massachusetts. Children's guide. Tower open Mon-Sat, 10am-4pm. Schools **Open all year.**

Boston (near), Boston Wash Banks, www.bostonwashbanks.com 01205 724678. A new conservation project involving the RSPB, linking various sites to give opportunities for walking and bird watching. Enjoy the tranquility of this area, perhaps join a guided walk or family event.

Grantham, Grantham Museum, St Peters Hill, 01476 568783. Explore the town's links with famous events and people, from Isaac Newton to Margaret Thatcher. Children's quiz sheets and holiday activities. Open daily, Mon-Sat, 10am-5pm. Schools **Open all year.**

Grimsby, The Peoples Park, Welholme Road. Relax in 26 acres of parkland with Victorian gardens and lake with wildfowl. Lots of grassy space for ball games and picnics. **Open all year.**
Town Hall Jail, 01472 324109. Explore and find out what life would have been like in the old prison cells and exercise yard. Open Mon-Thurs, 10am-3pm. Schools **Open all year.**

Hagworthingham (near), Stockwith Watermill, access from A158, 01507 588221. Follow the waymarked trails around the trout ponds and through wood and farmland. There are connections with Lord Tennyson who was born nearby. Tearoom. Open Mar–Oct, Tues-Sun and Bank Hol Mons, 10.30am-6pm; Nov-Dec, Thurs-Sun. **Open all year.**

Lincoln, Hartsholme Country Park and Swanholme Lakes, Skellingthorpe Road, 01522 873577. Popular park with woods, lakes, meadow and heaths. Visitor centre, café and ranger-led activities. Schools **Open all year.**
The Lawns, Union Road, 01522 873213. Adjacent to the castle, this area has various attractions including the Sir Joseph Banks Conservatory and the John Dawber Garden. Telephone TIC for opening times. Schools **Open all year.**

Lincoln (near), Whisby Nature Park, signposted from the A46 bypass, 01522 688868. Explore 365 acres of lakes, grassland and maturing scrub. Café and exhibition gallery in the Natural World Centre (small charge). Special events. Schools **Open all year.**

Louth, Hubbards Hills, 01507 609289. Accessed from the bypass, these hills drop into a deep valley with the meandering River Lud. Picnic, enjoy the open space or follow the Art Trail and find out about the Greenwich Meridian and Navigation Canal. Leaflets available from the TIC. **Open all year.**

Saltfleetby, Saltfleetby Dunes. Alongside the coast this National Nature Reserve has sand dunes, mud flats, and salt marsh. Excellent for wildlife and bird watching, but do follow the warning signs to avoid local dangers. **Open all year.**

Saxilby (near), Bransby Home of Rest for Horses, www.bransbyhorses.co.uk 01427 788464. Visit to see rescued horses, ponies and donkeys together with other farm animals. Open daily, 8am-4pm. Schools **Open all year.**

Scunthorpe, 20-21 Visual Arts Centre, St John's Church, Church Square, 01724 297070. This recently opened contemporary gallery has alternating exhibitions, and hands-on arts and craft activities for children. Open Tues-Sat, 10am-5pm. Schools **Open all year.**
North Lincolnshire Museum, Oswald Road, 01724 843533. If you are fascinated by geology and archaeology, search out the oldest exhibit which is some 200 million years old. Holiday activities. Open Tues-Sat, Bank Hol Mons, 10am-4pm, Sun, 1-4pm. Schools **Open all year.**
Steam Rail Tours, 01652 657053. Pre-book a free rail tour around Corus, hear the story of the great Victorian ironmasters and glimpse red-hot steel in the mills. Telephone for operational dates.

Skegness (near), Gibraltar Point, 01754 762677. This National Nature Reserve includes over 1,000 acres of sands, salt marsh and freshwater habitats. Waymarked paths, observation platform and bird hides. The visitor centre is open May-Oct, daily. Schools

Sleaford, Cogglesford Water Mill, East Road, 07966 400634. In an attractive setting, picnic, feed the ducks and explore the history of this ancient mill. Open Easter-Sept, Mon-Fri, 12noon-4pm, Sat-Sun and Bank Hol Mons, 11am-4.30pm; Oct-Mar, Sat-Sun, 12noon-4pm. Telephone for operational days (small charge). Schools **Open all year.**

Spalding, Ayscoughfee Hall Gardens, Churchgate, 01775 725468. Located behind the hall is a beautiful park with gardens, small play area, tennis, putting and café. A quiz sheet is available from the TIC.
Springfields Festival Gardens, www.springfields.mistral.co.uk 01775 724843. The spectacular annual flower parade through the town is on Sat 1st May. From this date, over 20 acres of redesigned gardens will re-open. Playground, carp lake and displays.

Spalding (near), Pinchbeck Engine and Land Drainage Museum, signposted off the A16 bypass, 01775 762715. A small site with working beam engine of the kind used to drain the Fens. Exhibition and picnic area. Open daily, Apr-Oct, 10am-4pm. Schools.

Spilsby (near), Snipe Dales Country Park, signposted off the B1195, 01507 526667. Enjoy waymarked trails across 200 acres of beautiful rolling countryside. Woods, ponds, streams and picnic areas. **Open all year.**

Stamford, Stamford Museum and Town Trail, Broad Street, 01780 766317. In one of the best-preserved stone towns of England meet Daniel Lambert and Tom Thumb, the largest and smallest of men. Follow the children's trail around the town and see an ancient almshouse. Holiday activities. Museum open Mon-Sat, 10am-5pm, Sun, 2-5pm, (Oct-Mar, closed Suns). Schools **Open all year.**

Woodhall Spa, Cottage Museum and Trail, Iddesleigh Road, 01526 353775. Learn about the spa waters and wartime connections, explore outside. Don't miss the huge Dambusters memorial. Open daily, Easter-late Oct, 10.30am-4.30pm. Schools.
Jubilee Park. Enjoy putting, tennis, paddling pool and outdoor swimming pool. For cycle hire check out 'Trips' chapter.

Wragby (near), Chambers Farm Wood, signposted off the B1202, 01623 822447. This extensive Forestry Commission woodland includes a National Nature Reserve and waymarked paths. **Open all year.**

NOTTINGHAMSHIRE

Clipstone (near), **Sherwood Pines Forest Park,** signposted off the B6030, 01623 822447. Enjoy the wonderful smell of pine in this, the largest forest open to the public, in the East Midlands. There are a variety of way marked paths and a choice of cycle routes to suit everyone from families to experienced off-roaders. A good adventure playground, Go Ape high-wire course (check out `Sports & Leisure' chapter), picnic areas, Ranger led activities and special events. Cycle hire available, shop and cafe open, Tues-Thurs, Sat & Sun, 10am-4pm. Park open daily, 8am-dusk. Schools **Open all year Check out page 12.**
Vicar Water Country Park, signposted off the B6030, 01623 466340. Walking and cycling along the Maun Valley trail and a large lake with day fishing available. Schools **Open all year.**

Eastwood, **D H Lawrence Birthplace Museum,** 8a Victoria Street, 01773 717353. This small house is an amazing time capsule of 1885, with no electricity or running water. The author's father was a coal miner and during the excellent guided tours you can hear stories of family life. Opening times as Durban House Heritage Centre.
Durban House Heritage Centre, Mansfield Road. An impressive building, originally the coal owners' offices where miners collected their wages. A variety of local history displays and a chance to have fun in the adjoining playground. Open daily, 10am-5pm (4pm Winter). Schools **Open all year.**

Edwinstowe, Sherwood Forest Country Park, www.sherwood-forest.org.uk 01623 823202. Beautiful ancient woodland with numerous waymarked paths. Find the 'Major Oak'. Children can collect 'Merry Men' stickers from various machines. The visitor centre is open daily, 10.30am-5pm (4.30pm Nov-Mar). Schools **Open all year.**

Langar, Naturescape Wildflower Farm, www.naturescape.co.uk 01949 860592. Follow the trail around fields planted with various wildflowers. Buy seeds for your own garden and picnic by the dragonfly pond. Open daily, Apr-Sept, 11am-5.30pm. Schools.

Langold, Langold Country Park, signposted off the A60, 01909 730189. Enjoy 400 acres with lake, woodland and playground. Fishing and rowing boats to hire (seasonal). **Open all year.**

Laxton, Laxton Visitor Centre, adjacent to the Dovecote Pub, 01777 871586. This attractive village retains a medieval strip-field system of farming. Watch a video and follow one of three trails. Pre-booked guided tours. Open daily, 9am-dusk. Schools **Open all year.**

Newark, Appletongate Museum, 01636 655740. Small local history collection with hands-on activities and a nursery rhyme trail. Roman lead coffins, 17th century swords and cannon balls! Open Mon-Wed, Fri-Sat, 10am-1pm, 2-5pm. Also Summer, Sun pm. Schools **Open all year.**
Newark Castle, 01636 678962. Impressive ruins alongside the River Trent. Across the castle gardens their story is retold in the Gilstrap Centre. Who are the two bejewelled figures and why are they significant here? In Summer, pre-booked guided tours of dungeons and tower (small charge). Open 9am-6pm (5pm Oct-Mar). Schools **Open all year.**
Riverside Park and Millgate Museum, 01636 655730. Take a boat trip, enjoy the playground and picnic opposite the castle ruins. Cross the river by the lock and find the old warehouse building converted into an excellent social history museum. Special events. Museum open Mon-Fri, 10am-5pm, Sat-Sun, Bank Hol Mons, 1-5pm. Schools **Open all year.**

Nottingham, Highfields Park, University Boulevard. This attractive open space has an extensive boating lake, children's playground and putting. **Open all year.**
National Water Sports Centre and Country Park, Holme Pierrepont, www.nationalsportscentres.co.uk 0115 982 1212. Enjoy a walk through 270 acres of parkland. There is usually activity on the international regatta course, man-made white water slalom or water-ski lagoon. Phone for details of courses available. **Open all year.**
Nottingham Museums. The following museums are normally free but a small charge may be made at weekends and during Bank Hols. Schools **Open all year.**
    Brewhouse Yard Museum, Castle Boulevard, 0115 915 3600. See 17th century cottages with an old shop, child's bedroom and a Victorian school. Trail goes into caves, formally used for storage and as air raid shelters. Open daily, 10am-4.30pm.
    Costume and Textile Museum, Castlegate, 0115 915 3500. Explore 200 years of costume displayed in a series of period room settings. Additional displays include Nottingham lace. Children's quiz sheets available. Open Wed-Sun, Bank Hols, 10am-4pm.
    Greens Mill, Windmill Lane, Sneinton, 0115 915 6878. Look around this fully operational windmill, once home of George Green, mathematician and physicist. Play with the hands-on science experiments. Open Wed-Sun, Bank Hol Mons, 10am-4pm.
    Nottingham Castle, Museum and Art Gallery, off Friar Lane, 0115 915 3700. The castle made famous by the story of Robin Hood is now a 17th century mansion with extensive exhibitions including a good interactive gallery. Descend 91m and visit Mortimers Hole, a series of underground passages (small charge). Outside, enjoy the gardens, themed playground and find the statue of Robin Hood. Open daily, 10am-5pm.
    Wollaton Hall and Park, Wollaton Road, 0115 915 3900. Extensive natural history displays are housed in this spectacular Tudor building. Lake, attractive gardens and deer park. Enjoy a picnic and follow 'George the Gorilla' around an eight-point trail. Hall open daily, 11am-5pm (4pm Winter). Park open daily, dawn-dusk.

Wollaton Hall Industrial Museum, Wollaton Road, 0115 915 3900, is located in the old stable block. Find displays about a wide range of industries from curtains to computers. See the miniature fairground, telephone exchange, ploughing and threshing machines. Telephone for dates of when working engines are in steam. Open daily, Apr-Sept, 11am-5pm.

Nottingham (near), **Bestwood Country Park,** located off the B683, 0115 927 3674. Woodland, heath and water meadow. In part grounds of a former large house, in part reclaimed colliery site. Find the old winding engine house. Ranger-led activities. Schools **Open all year.**

Ollerton (near), **Rufford Country Park,** 01623 822944. Enjoy 150 acres with lake, lots of wildfowl and woodland. Ranger-led activities. Visitor centre, craft centre and restaurant are open daily, 10.30am-5pm (shorter hours during Winter, telephone for details). Schools **Open all year.**

Ruddington, **Rushcliffe Country Park,** Mere Way, is 300 acres with many footpaths, a lake and good adventure playground. See steam trains pass as they travel from the Nottingham Transport Heritage Centre. **Open all year.**

Southwell, **Southwell Minster,** www.southwellminster.org.uk 01636 812649. In this impressive cathedral use the children's guide to find the carved mice, Roman painted fish, bread pews and stone carvings in the Chapter House. Adjacent visitor centre with video, exhibition and tearoom. Minster open daily. Schools **Open all year.**

Stoke Bardolph, **Severn Trent Education Centre,** Stoke Lane, 0115 989 6301. Opportunities to investigate water and waste management, study food chains and recycling links with the nearby dairy farm. Pre-booked school groups only. Schools **Open all year.**

Sutton-in-Ashfield (near), **Teversal Trails,** 01623 442021. There are numerous access points to this extensive network of paths and cycle routes along former railway lines. Nature trail, industrial history and a small visitor centre with a coal miner's garden. Schools **Open all year.**

Wales Bar, **Rother Valley Country Park,** Mansfield Road, 0114 247 1452, has four lakes, fishing, nature reserve, cycle hire and excellent watersports centre. Pitch and putt, playground, visitors centre and ranger-led activities. Open daily, dawn-dusk. Schools **Open all year.**

Welbeck (near), **Creswell Crags,** www.creswellcrags.org.uk 01909 720378. Limestone gorge with woodland and lake. A visitors centre with audiovisual displays and interactive computer programme is open daily, Feb-Oct, 10.30am-4.30pm, Nov-Jan, Sun only. Guided tours through caves once occupied by our ice-age ancestors (small charge) can be pre-booked on Sat-Sun, and daily during school hols. Schools **Open all year.**

Worksop (near), **Clumber Park,** NT, one mile from A1/A57, 01909 4765923. Landscaped grounds extending to 3,800 acres, with lake, woods, orienteering, fishing and special events. Also a Victorian walled garden and greenhouses (small charge and restricted opening, telephone for details). For cycle hire check out 'Trips' chapter. Schools **Open all year.**

RUTLAND

Clipsham, **Clipsham Wood.** Maintained by the Forestry Commission, this is a good place for walks and picnics. What shapes can you see clipped into the trees along the avenue up to Clipsham Hall? **Open all year.**

Oakham, **Rutland County Museum,** Catmos Street, 01572 758440. Exhibits include agricultural equipment, traditional rural crafts and some archaeological finds. Open Mon-Sat, 10am-5pm, Sun, 2-5pm (4pm Winter). Schools **Open all year.**

Oakham (near), **Rutland Water.** The largest man-made lake in Western Europe covers over 3,000 acres and from various access points you can go bird watching, try bank or boat fishing, enjoy a picnic, visit the adventure playground, try various watersports or the climbing wall, hire bikes or a rowing boat. Also boat trips. Schools **Open all year.**

History, Art & Science

Step back in time and find out about days gone by, or step forward and imagine yourself in the future. Art, history, science and technology find a place here. These places have admission charges, but there are many wonderful museums and places of interest which are free to visit. Check out the 'Free Places' chapter so you don't miss anything.

For opening times & prices at English Heritage sites please call 0870 333 1181or check out www.english-heritage.org.uk

East Midlands Quarries, www.qpa.org/playsafe 01491 410987. 'Play Safe – Stay Safe' education pack and details of how to arrange visits to a working quarry. Covers many aspects of the National Curriculum.

East Midlands Regimental Museums, 0115 985 4534, are in a variety of locations. The identity of each regiment is reflected in its uniform, medals, personal diaries, paintings and tableaux. Full details in a leaflet from East Midlands Museum Service.

DERBYSHIRE

Ashbourne (near), Sudbury Hall and Museum of Childhood, NT, 01283 585305. A 17th century house richly decorated, showing craftsmen's skills in wood and plaster work. In the museum discover how children worked and played in the past. Lots of hands-on activities. Picnic area. Open 20th Mar–31st Oct, Wed-Sun, Bank Hol Mons, 1-5pm. Schools Price B.

Bakewell, Bakewell Old House Museum, Cunningham Place, 01629 813642. Local history exhibits in a Tudor house, set amid narrow streets high above the parish church. Learn how the house was built using cow hair and dung. Discover a rare Tudor lavatory. Open daily, Apr-Oct. Phone for times. Schools Price A.

Bakewell (near), Chatsworth House, www.chatsworth.org 01246 582204. Follow the children's guide around this exceptional house with richly furnished rooms and a superb collection of art and sculpture. Enjoy the parkland and gardens with fountains, cascade and maze. Check out 'Farms' chapter. Open daily, 17th Mar-19th Dec, 11am-4.30pm. Schools Price C.

Haddon Hall, 01629 812855. A popular film and TV location, this medieval manor house has withstood the passage of time. See the old kitchens, banqueting hall, long gallery and terraced gardens. Open daily, 1st Apr-end Sept, 10.30am-4.30pm; Oct, Thurs-Sun, 10.30am-4pm. Schools Price B.

Belper, Derwent Valley Visitor Centre, www.belpernorthmill.org 01773 880474, is sited in North Mill, a hugely impressive industrial building. Watch a video, take a guided tour through the mill and discover the history of spinning cotton. Open Easter-Oct, Wed-Sun, 1-5pm, Nov-Easter, Thurs-Sun. Schools **Open all year** Price A.

Bolsover, Bolsover Castle, EH, 01246 822844. An impressive setting. Follow the audio tour to discover the various small rooms in the 17th century keep-like 'Little Castle'. Also an indoor riding school, one of the first of its kind. Special events. Phone for opening times. Schools **Open all year** Price B.

Buxton, Poole's Cavern, Green Lane, www.poolescavern.co.uk 01298 26978. Large natural cavern with spectacular formations, used by cave dwellers and the Romans. Visitor centre with limestone exhibition. Open daily, Mar-Oct, 10am-5pm. Schools Price B.

Castleton, Blue John Cavern, www.bluejohn.gemsoft.co.uk 01433 620638. On the underground guided tour, see rich deposits of Blue John. This is one of the few areas where this beautiful ornamental fluorspar is found. Also good stalactites and stalagmites. Open daily, 9.30am-5.30pm (dusk in Winter). Schools **Open all year** Price B.

Peak Cavern, www.peakcavern.co.uk 01433 620285. The people of the village used to live in the enormous entrance to this cave. For 400 years it was a centre of rope making. Open Easter-Oct, daily, 10am-4pm, Nov-Mar, Sat-Sun. Schools **Open all year** Price B.

Peak National Park Visitors Centre, 01433 620679. Opening in 2004 with interactive displays. Find out about local history, archaeology and geology. Phone for details.

Peveril Castle, 01433 620613, EH. See the impressive ruins, find out who William Peveril was, and what the connection was. Picnic and enjoy the outstanding views from this hill site. Children's activity sheets and special events. Phone for opening times. Schools **Open all year** Price A.

Speedwell Cavern, www.speedwellcavern.co.uk 01433 620512. The tour goes down 105 steps to an underground river. Boats depart every 15 minutes for the one-mile trip. Open daily, 10am-5pm (4pm Winter). Schools **Open all year** Price B.

Treak Cliff Cavern, www.bluejohnstone.com 01433 621487. These are mostly natural caverns, with excellent stalactites, stalagmites and flow stone formations. Also rich veins of Blue John. Open daily from 10am (Mar-Oct, last tour 4.20pm, Nov-Feb, 3.20pm). Schools **Open all year** Price B.

Chesterfield, The Crooked Spire, St Mary and All Saints, 01246 206506. A local landmark. The spire leans 2.9m from its true centre. Take a guided tour and climb up the tower. For details contact the Verger. Price A.

Chesterfield (near), Hardwick Hall, NT, Doe Lea, signposted from the M1, 01246 850430. This spectacular house was built for Bess of Hardwick, a friend of Queen Elizabeth I. Furniture, paintings, tapestries and fine gardens. Good children's guide, I-spy sheet and Stonemason's tour (Wed-Thurs). Open 31st Mar–31st Oct, Wed-Thurs, Sat-Sun and Bank Hol Mons, 12.30-4.30pm. Schools Price B.

Hardwick Old Hall, EH, 01246 850431. Adjacent to the 'new' Hall, these are impressive ruins and an early home of Bess of Hardwick. Audio tour and excellent children's guide. Phone for opening times. Schools Price A.

Stainsby Mill, NT, 01246 850430. Built in 1850 to grind flour for the Hardwick estate. Watch the massive waterwheel turn, try the children's I-spy sheet and enjoy a walk in the surrounding parkland. Phone for dates when mill operational. Schools Price A.

Denby, Denby Visitors Centre, www.denbyvisitorcentre.co.uk 01773 740799. Pre-book a factory tour and learn about the skills and stages involved in pottery production. Paint your own plate, have it fired and either return to collect or have it sent to you. Factory tours available Mon-Thurs. Also glass studio and cookery demonstrations. Schools **Open all year** Price B.

Derby, Royal Crown Derby, Osmaston Road, www.royal-crown-derby.co.uk 01332 712800. Take a pre-booked factory tour and see the various processes from raw material to finished fine china product. Demonstration studio and museum with outstanding collection of china, tracing the company's history over 250 years. Min age 10 years. Tours available Mon-Fri. **Open all year** Price B.

Derby (near), Kedleston Hall, NT, 01332 842191. Built to impress, this splendid classical Hall dominates the surrounding parkland. Lots of marble pillars, a glittering Indian collection and good children's guide. Open 20th Mar-end Oct, Sat-Wed, 12noon-4pm (parkland 11am-6pm). Schools Price B.

Shardlow Heritage Centre and Village Trail, off the A6, adjacent to Clock Warehouse family pub, 01332 792489. Discover the history of this unique 18th century inland port. Spot the old wharves and warehouses along the canal. Special events with hands-on activities. Open Easter-end Oct, Sat-Sun and Bank Hol Mons, 12noon-5pm. Schools Price A.

Eyam, Eyam Hall, www.eyamhall.com 01433 631976, is in the centre of the village. Take a guided tour around this 17th century home. Look at paintings, costumes and tapestries. Excellent hands-on group visits. Special events, craft centre and tearoom. Hall open May–end Aug, Wed-Thurs, Sun and Bank Hol Mons, 11am-4pm. Schools Price B.

Eyam Museum, Hawkhill Road, www.eyam.org.uk 01433 631371. See the dramatic story of the

Bubonic Plague outbreak of 1665-6 when the villagers quarantined themselves. Follow the harrowing tales of individual families and learn about the fleas and rats that carried the disease. See also, how the village recovered. Open 30th Mar-7th Nov, Tues-Sun and Bank Hol Mons, 10am-4.30pm. Schools Price A **Check out page 30.**

Matlock Bath, **Heights of Abraham,** www.heights-of-abraham.co.uk 01629 582365.
Cable car ride over the Derwent valley to the parkland high on the hillside. Enjoy the woodland trail, playground, cafe and picnic area. The guided tour underground through spectacular caves is not to be missed. Open daily, Easter-end Oct, 10am-5pm. Schools Price C.

Masson Mills, www.massonmills.co.uk 01629 581001. Built by Sir Richard Arkwright, this mill was his showpiece. Follow the bobbin trail and see lots of heavy textile machinery, some still in operation. Video and costumed guides. Open Mon-Fri, 10am-4pm, Sat, 11am-5pm, Sun, 11am-4pm. Schools **Open all year** Price A.

Peak District Mining Museum, www.peakmines.co.uk 01629 583834. Children will enjoy the various simulation climbing shafts as they learn about the history of the local lead mining industry. Opportunity to go underground at the Temple Mine or have a surface tour at the Magpie Mine. Telephone for details. Museum open daily, Apr-Oct, 10am-5pm, Nov-Mar, 11am-3pm. Schools **Open all year** Price B.

Melbourne, **Melbourne Hall and Gardens,** 01332 862502. The gardens have remained
virtually unchanged since the early 18th century. Look out for the yew tunnel, 'Birdcage', and various fountains. Find your favourite statue! Gardens open Apr-Sept, Wed, Sat-Sun and Bank Hol Mons, 1.30-5.30pm. House open Aug, Tues-Sun, 2-5pm. Telephone for prices.

Melbourne (near), **Calke Abbey,** Ticknall, NT, 01332 863822. An amazing house which
has been left in a state of disarray, just as it was found. See the impressive collections of stuffed birds, shells and fossils. The 750-acre parkland is glorious for walks. Special events include kite flying. House opens Easter-Oct, Sat-Wed, Bank Hol Mons, 1-5pm. Parkland open dawn-dusk. Schools Price B.

Renishaw, **Renishaw Hall and Gardens,** signposted off the A6135, 01246 432310. Enjoy
the wonderful trees and gardens which children can explore to find a lake, sculpture park and graves of family pets. History displays, crafts and tearoom in the stable block. Open 1st Apr-end Sept, Thurs-Sun and Bank Hol Mons, 10.30am-4pm. Price A/B.

Rowsley, **Caudwell's Mill,** 01629 734374, is attractively situated alongside the river. Look at
amazing machinery on four floors of this large Victorian water turbine-powered roller flour mill. Also hands-on models, nature trail, craft workshops and cafe. Open daily, 9.30am-5pm. Schools **Open all year** Price B.

South Wingfield, **Wingfield Manor,** EH, 01773 832060. Enjoy an audio tour around
superb ruins where Mary, Queen of Scots, was frequently imprisoned. Take care with the off-road parking and walk up a track across farmland. Phone for opening times. Schools **Open all year** Price A.

Tissington, **Tissington Hall,** 5 miles N of Ashbourne, 01335 352200, is located in a picture-
postcard village. Enjoy a guided tour around this beautiful Jacobean manor house, the home of the Fitzherbert family for 500 years. Children over 10 years only. Open Jun-Aug, Mon-Fri, afternoons. Telephone for prices.

Wirksworth, **Wirksworth Heritage Centre,** Crown Yard, 01629 825225, has displays with
a computer game 'Rescue the injured lead miner'. Also walk through the cave-maze which starts with finding a prehistoric woolly rhino. Phone for opening times. Schools Price A.

Wirksworth (near), **National Stone Centre,** www.nationalstonecentre.org.uk 01629
824833. Displays with children's quiz sheet explaining geology, quarrying and use of stone. Outside trails around fossil limestone, gem panning and a 'unique' wall built using stones from different regions. Open daily, 10am-5pm (4pm Winter). Schools **Open all year** Price A.

LEICESTERSHIRE

Ashby-de-la-Zouch, Ashby Castle, EH, South Street, 01530 413343. Follow the audio tour around this impressive ruin. Climb the massive tower, explore the underground passage, take a picnic and enjoy games on the grass. Special events include medieval pageantry. Phone for opening times. Schools **Open all year** Price A.

Belvoir, Belvoir Castle, signposted off the A607, www.belvoircastle.com 01476 870262. This popular film location has fine state rooms, an interactive Regency nursery, beautiful grounds, an adventure playground and special events featuring medieval jousting. Open Apr-Sept, Tues-Thurs, Sat-Sun and Bank Hol Mons; Mar and Oct, Suns, 11am-5pm. Schools Price C.

Castle Donington, The Donington Grand Prix Collection, signposted off the A453, www.doningtoncollection.com 01332 811027, is adjacent to the motor racing circuit. See the world's largest collection of Grand Prix racing cars. With memorabilia and videos, the history of motor racing is retold. Open daily, 10am-4pm. Schools **Open all year** Price B.

Coalville, Snibston Discovery Park, Ashby Road, 01530 510851. Local industrial heritage and extensive hands-on science displays. Outside interactive 'water experiments' (Summer only) and science playground, train ride, nature trail, fishing and special events. Why not join a guided tour around the former colliery pit top? Open daily, 10am-5pm. Schools **Open all year** Price B.

Foxton, Foxton Canal Museum and Country Park, www.foxton.org.uk 0116 279 2657. Explore a flight of ten locks, investigate the remains of a steam- powered boat lift and walk along the Grand Union canal. Take a picnic or enjoy a boat trip. Museum open daily, Easter-Oct, 10am-5pm; Winter, phone for details. Schools **Open all year** Price A.

Leicester, The Challenger Learning Centre, 0870 607 7223, is adjacent to the National Space Centre. Enjoy realistic space simulations, wear mission uniforms, communication headsets and sit at electronic workstations. This is the only centre of its kind outside the USA (age 9+). Mainly for pre-booked groups but phone for details of occasional public open Sats. Schools **Open all year.**
National Space Centre, www.spacecentre.co.uk 0870 607 7223. In this futuristic structure find an international collection of space artefacts, including rocket engines and spacesuits. Lots of hands-on activities. Don't miss the film in the Space Theatre. Phone for opening details. Schools **Open all year** Price C.

Loughborough, Bell Foundry, Freehold Street, www.taylorbells.co.uk 01509 233414. The bell for St Paul's in London was made here. The museum with good children's guide is open Tues-Fri and Summer Sats, 10am-12.30pm and 1.30-4.30pm. Telephone for details of foundry tours when it might be possible to watch molten metal being poured and a new bell cast. Schools **Open all year** Price A/B.
Carillon and War Museum, Queens Park, 01509 263370. Climb the tower, see the 47 bells of the carillon and good views over the town. On Thurs and Sats it's possible to listen to the carillon being played. Find out why there is a war museum here. Open Good Fri-end Sept, daily. Phone for details. Schools Price A.

Loughborough (near), Beaumanor Hall, Woodhouse, 01509 890119. Visited mainly by schools and other children's groups. Experience life in a Victorian classroom and find out what the Hall was used for during the War. Sport, nature study and Summer holiday activities. Schools.

Lutterworth (near), Stanford Hall, 2 miles from the A14/M6/M1 junction, www.stanfordhall.co.uk 01788 860250. See the fine paintings and discover why there is a replica of an 1898 flying machine. Also a motorbike museum. Open Easter-end Sept, Sun and Bank Hol Mons, 1.30-5pm. Special events. Schools Price B.

Market Bosworth (near), **Bosworth Battlefield Visitor Centre,** Sutton Cheney 01455 290429, is at the historic site of the Battle of Bosworth Field 1485, where King Richard III was defeated by the future King Henry VII. This famous battle is brought to life with splendid models of the scene of battle, life size soldiers in full armour and an exhibition about weaponry and wounds. Watch a video before exploring outside to follow the battle trails across fields. Look out for the display boards and huge flags (weather dependent) indicating the approach route of the various forces. Near the Ashby Canal find the stone which marks the spot where King Richard III was killed. Visit Sutton Cheney church where King Richard was said to have taken mass for the last time. Special events include battle re-enactment, and falconry (extra charge). The Visitor Centre is open Apr-Oct, daily, 11am-5pm, Nov-Dec, Suns, 11am-4pm, Mar, Sat-Sun, 11am-5pm. Pre-booked groups all year. Battle trails open all year. Schools Price A **Check out page 30**.

Moira, **Moira Furnace and Country Park,** 01283 224667. Sign posted off B5003, this is the best preserved iron smelting furnace in Britain. Situated alongside a newly re-watered stretch of the Ashby canal, the whole area is landscaped with woodland, display boards and heritage trail. Take a guided tour inside the furnace building, and enjoy the hands-on activities. Also boat trip, extensive playground, craft units and cafe. Special events and Sunday Fundays. Museum open, Apr-Aug, Tues-Sun, and Bank Hol Mons, 11am-5pm; Sept-Mar, Wed-Sun, 11am-4pm. Grounds open daily, dawn-dusk. Schools Birthdays **Open all year** Price B **Check out page 30**.

Wigston, **Framework Knitters' Museum,** Bushloe End, near the church, www.knittingtogether.org.uk 0116 288 3396. Don't miss this 'time capsule' on the outskirts of Leicester. A small house, it has a workshop with eight hand frames. Open 1st Sat in month and every Sun, 2-5pm. Schools Price A.

LINCOLNSHIRE

Aviation Heritage, 01522 526450. From the Dambusters to the Red Arrows, Lincolnshire is renowned as the 'Home of the Royal Air Force'. There are many airfield sites to visit. See historic aircraft, a wartime operation room and memorial books. Have a go on simulation flight decks and enjoy various airshows. Leaflets available from the TIC.

Windmills, 01522 528448. There are 17 working windmills in Lincolnshire. The variety includes the highest in the country, one with unusual left-handed sails, an early postmill and one in the centre of Lincoln. On certain days it's possible to explore inside, buy flour or relax in a tearoom. Take part in the Windmill Passport scheme and collect a stamp from each mill visited. Phone for details.

Alford, **Alford Windmill,** East Street, 01507 462136. Full of atmosphere. Climb ladders to see six floors of this excellent windmill and explore the centuries-old stone grinding process. Open daily, Jul-Sept; Oct, Tues, Fri-Sun; Nov-Mar, Tues, Sat-Sun; Apr-Jun, Tues, Fri-Sun, 10am-5pm (open Suns 11am). Schools Price A.

Manor House Museum, West Street, 01507 463073. Relax in the tea garden at the rear of England's largest thatched manor house. The museum has extensive local history displays. Open Easter-Sept, Mon-Sat, 10.30am-4.30pm, Sun, 12noon-4pm. Schools Price A.

Bourne (near), **Grimesthorpe Castle,** www.grimsthorpe.co.uk 01778 591205, is set in 3,000 acres of parkland. Henry VIII once stayed in this incredible house. Explore on foot, by cycle or Land Rover tour. See the red deer, lakes, gardens and enjoy the adventure playground. Phone for opening times. Schools Price B.

Colsterworth (near), **Woolsthorpe Manor,** NT, 01476 860338. This small 17th century house was the birthplace and home of Isaac Newton. Picnic in the orchard, a reminder of the famous apple tree. Also interactive science exhibition and countryside walks. Special events. Open Mar and Oct, Sat-Sun, 1-5pm; Apr-Sept, Wed-Sun and Bank Hol Mons, 1-5pm. Schools Price A.

Learn all about

The Plague!

at EYAM MUSEUM

Find out about Bubonic Plague in the Peak District village where it killed over a third of the population in 1665/6. Learn about the black rats, the fleas that carried the disease, and see the stories of the families it affected.
See how the village recovered afterwards.

Hawkhill Rd, Eyam, Derbyshire

Just off the A623. Signposted in the village.

Open Tuesday - Sunday (and Bank Holidays)
from 30th March - 7th November 2004

Tel: 01433 631371.

MOIRA FURNACE

A BLAST FROM THE PAST TO FIRE YOUR IMAGINATION!

The Furnace is a spectacular brick structure completed in 1806. Now a scheduled Ancient Monument it houses a fascinating, hands-on exhibition, with talking models, computer graphics, experiments, sounds and light effects. See how iron making developed and why the building survives today.

Other Attractions incudes Lime Kilns, Woodland Plantation Boardwalk, Playground, Canal (including Boat Trips), Gift Shop, Tea Room, Craft Units.

Location - Moira Furnace is on Furnace Lane, off the Shortheath Road (B5003), Moria, Nr Ashby de la Zouch, Leicestershire. Moira is situated at the Heart of the National Forest and nearby are a range of places to visit.

OPENING TIMES

Summer: 1 April - 31 August: Tues - Fri 12.30 - 5.00pm
Sat, Sun & Bank Hols: 11.30am - 5.00pm
Winter: 1 September - 31 March: Wed - Fri 12.30 - 4.00pm
Sat & Sun 11.30am - 4.00pm
Closed Christmas Day, Boxing Day & New Years Day
Admission charge for Furnace only
£3 Adults, £2 Concessions, £1 Children
Telephone: 01283 224667

www.leics.gov.uk   Leicestershire County Council

Bosworth Battlefield

Visitor Centre & Country Park

Visit the site of the Battle of Bosworth Field where in 1485 Richard III lost his life and crown to the future Henry VII.

Visitor Centre open 11am to 5pm 1st April to 31st October. Film Theatre. Book and Gift Shop. Battle trail open all year. Special Events. Medieval weekend 21/22 August (including battle re-enactment). Pre-booked groups all year. Group rates available.

For information phone 01455 290429.

Bosworth Battlefield Visitor Centre & Country Park, Sutton Cheney, Nuneaton, CV13 0AD. Email: bosworth@leics.gov.uk

Coningsby, Battle of Britain Memorial Flight, 01526 344041. On a guided tour see an impressive collection of heritage planes. The visitor centre has a wartime exhibition and café. Outside enjoy the viewing area alongside the active RAF runway (very noisy). Tours on Mon-Fri, 10.30am-3.30pm (Winter 3pm). Schools **Open all year** Price A.

Dorrington (near) North Ings Farm Museum, off B1188, 01526 833100. Collections include old agricultural machinery including several vintage tractors. Take a ride on the narrow-gauge railway which used to convey materials around the farm. Open Apr-Oct, first Sun in the month, 10am-5pm. Price A.

East Kirkby, Lincolnshire Aviation Heritage Centre, www.lincsaviation.co.uk 01790 763207. On this old airfield site see a variety of military vehicles, masses of memorabilia and the enormous Avro Lancaster Bomber. Original control tower, air raid shelter and memorial chapel. Open Mon-Sat, 10am-5pm (4pm Winter). Schools **Open all year** Price B.

Epworth, Epworth Old Rectory, 01427 872268. The birthplace of John Wesley, founder of Methodism. During the guided tour find out what sort of childhood he had. Ponder on his mother's parenting skills. Open Mar-Apr and Oct, Mon-Sat, 10am-12noon, 2-4pm, Sun, 2-4pm; May-Sept, 10am-4.30pm, Sun, 2-4.30pm. Schools Price A.

Gainsborough, Gainsborough Model Railway, Florence Terrace, 01427 615871. If you are a fan of model railways, track down this extensive 'O'-gauge model. Based on the East Coast main line c1940, it is one of the largest models of its type in the country. Phone for opening dates. Price A.

Gainsborough Old Hall, EH, Parnell Street, 01427 612669. This timber-framed medieval manor house seems totally out of place in the modern town centre. Explore with an audio tour and learn how King Richard III and Henry VIII both stayed here. Special events. Phone for opening times. Schools **Open all year** Price A.

Grantham (near), Belton House, NT, 01476 566116. An impressive house with fine furniture, paintings and tapestries. There are 1,000 acres of parkland with an excellent adventure playground and formal gardens. Open 31st Mar-31st Oct, Wed-Sun and Bank Hol Mons, 12.30-5pm. Gardens, 11am-5.30pm. Schools Price B.

Grimsby, National Fishing Heritage Centre, Alexandra Dock, 01472 323345. Often described as one of the toughest jobs in the world, this award winning centre invites you to sign on as a crew member for a journey of discovery, taking you to the edge of disaster and the extremes of the elements. Follow the trail through exhibition areas, small rooms, winding passageways, never knowing what the next door will open into. Use the navigation maps and equipment on the boat to travel to the Arctic fishing grounds. Experience the rolling seas, the urgency and excitement of the catch, the raw blasts of the winds, cramped living conditions and the heat of the engine room. It was a hard life on board, but the Centre also shows what life was like on shore, at home and in the local pub. Remember to get a timed ticket to go on board the fishing boat moored adjacent to the Centre. Explore inside and imagine what it would be like out at sea. Then return to the Centre for refreshments. Souvenirs are available in the gift shop. Open Mon-Fri, 10am-5pm, Sat-Sun and Bank Hol Mons, 10.30am-5.30pm. Schools **Open all year** Price B **Check out inside front cover.**

Heckington, Heckington Windmill and Railway Museum, 01529 414294. Children will enjoy climbing the mill and finding working railway models in the museum opposite. Phone TIC for opening times of each attraction. Price A.

Lincoln, Lincoln Castle, 01522 511068. William the Conqueror's castle dates from 1068. Walk the castle walls and see one of only four surviving copies of the Magna Carta. Also a Victorian prison chapel, guided tours and special events including jousting. Open Mon-Sat, 9.30am-4.30pm, Sun, 11am-5.30pm (3.30pm Winter). Schools **Open all year** Price A.

Lincoln Cathedral, www.lincolncathedral.com 01522 544544. One of Europe's finest Gothic buildings. Explore independently or pre-book a children's guided tour. Open daily, 7am-8pm (6pm Winter). Schools **Open all year** Price A.

Medieval Bishop's Old Palace, EH, Minster Yard, 01522 527468. Climb the stairs of the tower, explore the vaulted undercroft, the garden and one of the most northerly vineyards in Europe. Audio tour available. Phone for opening times. Schools **Open all year** Price A.

Museum of Lincolnshire Life, Burton Road, 01522 528448. Situated in old army barracks, this is now an award-winning social history museum. Lots of hands-on opportunities. Don't forget to see the Ellis Windmill which is nearby. Museum open daily, May-Oct, 10am-5.30pm; Nov-Apr, Mon-Sat, 10am-5.30pm, Sun, 2-5.30pm. Schools **Open all year** Price A.

Lincoln (near), Doddington Hall, 01522 694308. A superb Elizabethan mansion, a family home set in six acres of attractive gardens with gatehouse and family church. Gardens only, open 16th Feb-27th Apr, Sun, 2-6pm. House and gardens open 2nd May–26th Sept, Wed, Sun, Bank Hol Mons, 2-6pm. Schools Price A/B.

Navenby, Mrs Smith's Cottage, 3 East Road, on the A607, 01529 414294. A remarkable survival of a bygone age. Find out about Mrs Smith who lived until she was 102 years old. As the cottage is tiny, pre-booking is recommended. Phone for details from the TIC. Schools Price A.

Scunthorpe (near), Normanby Hall and Country Park, 01724 720588. Enjoy 300 acres of parkland with horse and pony rides, nature trails, miniature railway, and adventure playground. Also costume galleries, farming museum and Victorian walled gardens. Special events. House open daily, Apr-Sept, 1-5pm. Parkland and gardens open all year, dawn-dusk. Schools Price A.

Sibsey, Sibsey Trader Windmill, EH, 5 miles N of Boston, www.sibsey.fsnet.co.uk 01205 460647. This is an impressive mill. Explore six storeys to learn about the working machinery. Tearoom and organic flour for sale. Phone for opening times. Price A.

Skegness, Church Farm Museum, Church Road South, 01754 766658. A complex of buildings set around a grassy area that give a suggestion of traditional farmlife. Special events. Open daily, Apr-Oct, 10.30am-5.30pm. Schools Price A.

Spalding, Gordon Boswell Romany Museum, signposted from the A16 bypass, 01775 710599. In an authentic setting find all manner of memorabilia including several Romany vardos (gypsy caravans.) Pre-book a day out in a horse-drawn vardo with a meal cooked over a traditional fire. Open Easter-Oct, Thurs-Sun, 10.30am-5pm. Schools Price B.

Spilsby (near), Gunby Hall, NT, off the A158, 01909 486411. Attractively situated, this 18th century country house has walled flower and kitchen gardens. The red brick house has been likened to many a dolls house! Open 31st Mar-29th Sept, Wed, 2-6pm. Gardens only, Thurs, 2-6pm. Price A/B.

Stamford (near), Burleigh House, www.burghley.co.uk 01780 752451. A magnificent Elizabethan house with amazing painted ceilings and state rooms. Find memorabilia from the Olympic gold medallist, Lord Burghley. Also deer park, lakeside walks, sculpture garden and annual horse trials. Open daily, Apr-Oct, 11am-5pm. Schools Price B.

Tattershall, Tattershall Castle, NT, 01526 342543. An impressive brick tower which can be seen from miles around. Picnic, climb the battlements, and with the audio guide imagine what it was like in medieval times. Guardhouse museum and moat. Special events. Open Mar, Sat-Sun, 12noon-4pm; Apr-Oct, Sat-Wed, 11am-5.30pm (Oct till 4.30pm); Nov-Dec, Sat-Sun, 12noon-4pm. Schools Price A.

Watham, Watham Windmill, 01472 822236. Climb the mill, visit craft shops and the small rural life museum. Enjoy the children's play area and take a ride on the miniature train. Tearoom and picnic area. Special events. Phone for opening times. Schools Price A.

NOTTINGHAMSHIRE

Laxton, Beth Shalom Holocaust Centre, www.holocaustcentre.net 01623 836627. Set within a quiet memorial garden, the centre houses a sensitive yet powerful exhibition outlining the history and tragic destruction of Europe's Jews by the Nazis. Suitable for children over 12 years. Open Feb-Nov, Wed-Sun, 10am-5pm (daily in Aug). Schools **Open all year** Price B.

Mansfield, Making It! Discovery Centre, www.makingit.org.uk 01623 473297. Ever wondered how things are made? An award-winning attraction with excellent hands-on exhibits. Assemble your own working model and take it home as a souvenir. Open daily, 10am-last admission 3.15pm. Schools Birthdays **Open all year** Price B.

Newark (near), Newark Air Museum, Winthorpe Aerodrome, www.newarkairmuseum.co.uk 01636 707170. A diverse display of over 50 aircraft, from bi-planes to bombers. Look out for the 1938 Flying Flea! Indoor exhibits showing engines, radios and uniforms. Open daily, 10am-5pm (4pm Nov-Feb). Schools **Open all year** Price B.

Vina Cooke Museum of Dolls and Bygone Childhood, The Old Rectory, Cromwell, 01636 821364. Every room in this 17th century house is crammed with dolls and toys from many different eras. Open Mon-Thurs, 10.30am-12noon, 2-5pm, Sat-Sun, 10.30am-5pm. Phone to check Winter opening. Schools **Open all year** Price A.

Nottingham, City of Caves, Broadmarsh Shopping Centre, www.cityofcaves.com 0115 988 1955, is located in the heart of the city. Descend right under the modern shopping centre. As part of the surprise, discover what these sandstone caves were once used for. Open daily, 10.30am-4pm. Schools **Open all year** Price B.

Galleries of Justice, High Pavement, www.galleriesofjustice.org.uk 0115 952 0555. An award-winning museum with much to see and take part in. Over 250 years of history, located in and around an original courthouse, county gaol and 1905 police station. Open Tues-Sun, Bank Hol Mons and school hol Mons, 10am-5pm (4pm Nov-Mar). Schools **Open all year** Price B.

The Tales of Robin Hood, Maid Marion Way, www.robinhood.uk.com 0115 948 3284. In this Centre children will love to explore the story of Robin Hood. How much of it is based on fact, how much is fiction? You make up your own mind. First, in uniquely designed cars travel back in time to experience the sights, sounds and smells of medieval England. Then follow the trail of the Silver Arrow. Children can practise archery and become an honorary outlaw. Filmshow and themed cafe. Open daily, 10am-4.30pm. Schools Birthdays **Open all year** Price B **Check out page 34.**

Papplewick, Papplewick Pumping Station, off Longdale Road, www.papplewickpumpingstation.co.uk 0115 963 2938. A Victorian waterworks with massive James Watt beam engines. Also a steam-powered forge, passenger-carrying miniature railway and model boat display on the lake. Phone for dates of when in steam. Schools Price A.

Ratcliffe, Ratcliffe Power Station, off the A453, 0115 936 5000. See the huge cooling towers, computer room, and mounds of coal and rail tracks. Informative, but in places noisy. Hard hats and ear protectors are provided. Pre-booked school visits only (age 10+). Schools.

Ravenshead, Newstead Abbey, signposted off A60, 01623 455900. Initially an abbey and later the home of Lord Byron, this large house has extensive parkland with lakes, gardens and a children's playground. Special events. House open daily, Apr-Sept, 12noon-5pm. Parkland open all year, 9.30am-dusk. Schools Price A.

Ruddington, Framework Knitters' Museum, Chapel Street, www.rfkm.org 0115 984 6914, is set in a Victorian courtyard. Look around the tiny cottages and see the framework knitters' machines. Video, demonstration and hands-on opportunities. Special events. Open Easter-Dec, Wed-Sat and Bank Hol Mons, 11am-4.30pm, also Easter-Sept, Suns, 1.30-4pm. Schools Price A.

Southwell, Southwell Workhouse, NT, 01636 8172500. Was this institution for the poor and destitute really the harsh prison painted by many a Victorian novel? Follow the children's trail,

'Master's Punishment' game and audio tour around this large building and make up your own mind. Open 29th Mar–2nd Nov, Thurs-Mon, 12noon-5pm (11am Aug). Schools Price B.

Tuxford, **Walks of Life Exhibition,** 01777 870427. A collection of vehicles which rely totally on human muscle power for their movement. Can you find the fire fighting vehicles, the water carts, a seed drill, and street piano? Open Apr-Oct, Wed, Sun and Bank Hol Mons, 2-6pm. Groups all year, by prior arrangement. Schools Price A.

Upton, **British Horological Institute,** www.bhi.co.uk 01636 813795. See an amazing collection of clocks and watches in an old manor house. Find the first 'speaking clock' and the Greenwich Time '6 pips' equipment. Perhaps more suitable for older children. Open last Sun in Mar–end Oct, Sat-Sun and Bank Hol Mons. Schools Price B.

Worksop, **Mr Straw's House,** NT, 7 Blyth Grove, 01909 482380. This semi-detached house is an amazing time capsule of the 1920-30s. Find out about Mr Straw, a local grocer and bachelor who did little to alter the house after his parents died. Video and exhibits to handle. Please book a timed ticket in advance. Open Apr-Oct, Tues-Sat, 11am-4.30pm. Schools Price B.

RUTLAND

Oakham (near), **Normanton Church Museum,** Rutland Water, 01572 653026. In a small church which juts out into the water, this museum tells of the construction of the reservoir including the discovery of some human skeletons and fossils. Open Easter-Oct, most days. Phone TIC for details. Schools Price A.

Uppingham (near), **Rockingham Castle,** 01536 770240, was built by William the Conqueror. There are only three Norman castles on this scale remaining in England and it is only here that the original layout can be seen. The castle is situated on the borders of four counties. Children's information sheets. Phone for opening details. Schools Price B.

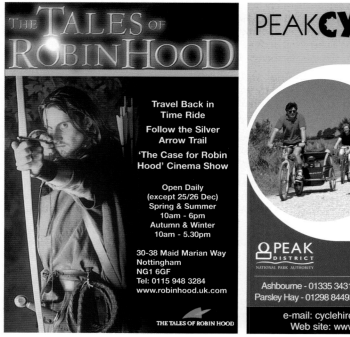

Trips & Transport

Journey by using your own muscle power - get fit and cycle! Or explore the waterways and hire a boat! To take things more leisurely go on a boat trip with commentary and perhaps a meal. For another idea to get away from the car, try a bus trip or soak up the atmosphere with a ride on a steam railway. For something extra special, experience the age of tram or trolley bus.

BOAT HIRE

Boats are usually available Summer months only, by the hour or half hour.

DERBYSHIRE

Belper, 01773 841415. From the riverside gardens hire a rowing boat on the River Derwent.
Chesterfield. There are rowing boats on the lake in Queens Park.
Derby, 01332 343075. In Markeaton Park children can enjoy the canoes at Mundy Play Centre or the whole family can share a rowing boat.
Matlock. Try the super-fun small motor boats on the lake in Hall Leys Park.
Matlock Bath. Rowing boats on the River Derwent.
Wirksworth (near), 01629 540478. A variety of boats including canoes and rowing boats available from a busy centre on Carsington Water.

LEICESTERSHIRE

Barrow-on-Soar, Barrow Boating, Mill Lane, www.barrowboating.co.uk 01509 415001. Rowing boats and pedaloes on the River Soar.
Leicester. Rowing boats on the lake in Abbey Park.
Market Bosworth, Bosworth Water Trust, 01455 291876. On the lake hire a canoe, a kayak or go sailing. Tuition available.
Melton Mowbray (near), Twin Lakes, 01664 567777. As part of a visit to Twin Lakes adventure park enjoy the rowing boats and pedaloes.

LINCOLNSHIRE

Boston, Boston Marina, 01205 364420. On the River Witham hire a self-drive motor boat for the day or per hour.
Cleethorpes, Humber Estuary Discovery Centre, 01472 323232. Relax on the lake in a rowing boat.
Lincoln, Lincoln Boat Trips, www.lincolnboattrips.com 07970 942801. Hire a 2-8 person, self-drive motor boat from Brayford Pool and explore the Fossdyke Roman canal.
Mablethorpe. Rowing boats and pedaloes on the lake in Queens Park, off the Central Promenade.
Skegness. Pedaloes on the boating lake off South Parade.

NOTTINGHAMSHIRE

Langold, Langold Country Park, 01909 730189. Rowing boats on the lake.
Nottingham. Rowing boats on the extensive boating lake in Highfields Park, off University Bouvelard.
Wales Bar, Rother Valley Country Park, 0114 247 1453. A variety of craft on the lakes, including rowing boats. A popular watersports centre.

RUTLAND

Oakham (near), 01780 460154. Rowing boats available on the north shore of Rutland Water.

BOAT HIRE (NARROW BOATS)

Hire a self-steer narrow boat for a day or half day. The boats accommodate 6-12 persons. Good for a family picnic or birthday party. No previous experience is required as brief instruction is given.

LEICESTERSHIRE

Barrow-on-Soar, Barrow Boating, www.barrowboating.co.uk 01509 415001. Explore Charnwood from the River Soar, pass through locks, watch wildlife and relax.

Foxton, Foxton Boat Services, www.foxtonboats.co.uk 0116 279 2285. Having explored Foxton Locks on foot, travel by boat through picturesque countryside along the Grand Union Canal.

Market Harborough, Union Wharf Narrowboats, 01858 432123. Cruise a lock-free section of the Grand Union Canal from the newly developed Harborough Basin towards Foxton Locks.

Market Harborough (near), Kilworth Wharf Leisure, 01858 880484. Cruise a lock-free section of the Grand Union Canal. Time to pause for a picnic and visit Foxton locks.

Sileby, Sileby Mill Boatyard, www.silebymill.co.uk 01509 813583. Enjoy passing through locks along the River Soar towards Loughborough or south through Watermead Country Park.

Stoke Golding, Ashby Boat Company, www.ashbyboats.co.uk 01455 212671. Cruise on the picturesque lock-free Ashby Canal and pass the site of Bosworth Battlefield.

BOAT TRIPS

Let someone else take charge, sit back, relax and listen to the commentary. Perhaps learn something about local history and wildlife.

DERBYSHIRE

Castleton, 01433 620512. One-mile underground trip through Speedwell Cavern, an old flooded lead mine. Operates daily. Check out 'History' chapter.

Chesterfield, Chesterfield Canal Trust, www.chesterfield-canal-trust.org.uk 01246 551035. Enjoy a 45-minute trip along the Chesterfield Canal on the narrow boat 'John Varley'. It operates Easter-Nov, Sun and Bank Hol Mons. Also Santa Specials. The boat is available for charter, max 12 passengers.

Derby (near), www.stensonbubble.com 01283 703113. From Stenson village the electrically-powered 'Stenson Bubble' runs 2 or 3 hour trips along the River Trent. Meals are available on board. Telephone for dates.

Whaley Bridge, 01663 734737. Along the Peak Forest Canal on the restaurant boat 'Judith Mary'. Cruise lasts 2.5 hours. Telephone for dates.

LEICESTERSHIRE

Foxton, Foxton Boat Services, 0116 279 2285. Afternoon trips on a motor launch along Grand Union Canal, Easter-Sept, Sat-Sun and Bank Hol Mons. More frequently during Summer school hols. Horse-drawn narrow-boat trip available for pre-booked groups.

Leicester, Swan Line Cruises, 0116 251 2334. The 'Duke of Bridgewater' narrow boat operates on the River Soar between the National Space Centre and Abbey Park. Sometimes longer trips towards Watermead Country Park. The boat is also available for charter. Min party size 25. Phone for details including Santa Specials.

Moira, 01283 224667. From opposite the Moira Furnace the 'Joseph Wilkes' narrowboat offers a 20 minute trip on a stretch of the re-watered Ashby Canal. **Check out 'History' chapter and page 30.**

Sutton Cheney, The Ashby Trip, www.ashbytrip.com 01455 213838. On the Ashby Canal, the 'Rosebud' offers a 20-minute water-bus service to and from Bosworth Battlefield. The narrow boat 'Jubilee' offers one-hour trips. There is also a themed restaurant boat, 'The Rose'. Telephone for times and details including Santa Specials.

LINCOLNSHIRE

Boston, Maritime Leisure Cruises, 01205 460595. Enjoy a full-day sea trip on the 'Mystere' to find seals on the sand banks in the Wash. The 'Boston Belle' offers a shorter sea trip or a variety of river cruises. Telephone for timetable. Both boats are also available for private charter.

Brigg, Phoenix Boat Trips, 07949 741094. Relax on a 45-minute trip on 'Firefly', an open boat on the River Ancholme. Dependent on weather conditions, it operates Apr-Oct, Mon-Sat.

Lincoln, Lincoln Boat Trips, 01522 881200, or **Cathedral City Cruises,** 01522 546853. On either the double-decker 'Brayford Belle' or the fully enclosed 'City of Lincoln', enjoy a 45-minute cruise from Brayford Pool, along the Fossdyke Roman canal. Available daily, Easter-Oct. Both boats are available for charter.

Stamford, 01780 755611. Telephone the TIC for details of a one-hour chartered trip on a chauffeured punt along the River Welland. Mon-Fri evenings, and Sat-Sun, 1-6pm.

NOTTINGHAMSHIRE

Newark, The Newark Line, 01636 525246. On the River Trent, 1 or 1_ hour afternoon trips on 'River Prince' or 'The Sonning'. Operates Easter-Oct with daily trips during Summer hols. The boats are also available for charter.

Nottingham, Princess River Cruises, www.princessrivercruises.co.uk 0115 910 0400. Enjoy a two or three hour round trip from Trent Bridge, along the River Trent towards Newark. Meals are available on board. The large boat 'Nottingham Princess' has daily sailings. Look out for children's themed events including Santa trips. Telephone for timetable.

Nottingham (near), www.trentcruising.com 0115 910 0507. Explore the River Trent on a Sunday Lunch Cruise leaving from the Park Yacht Inn, Colwick. The refurbished 'Trent Lady' also runs Santa trips and is available for charter, min 25 passengers.

Ranby, Chesterfield Canal Trust, www.chesterfield-canal-trust.org.uk Pre-book a Sunday afternoon trip along the Chesterfield Canal on the 'Norwood Packet'. Operates Easter-Oct. Or charter the boat for a birthday party, max 12 passengers, Pre-booked Santa Specials also available.

Sawley, near Long Eaton, 01509 813311. Boat available for charter for trips along the Rivers Trent and Soar. Min party size 25.

RUTLAND

Oakham (near), Rutland Water Cruises, www.rutlandwatercruises.com 01572 787630. From Whitwell harbour enjoy a cruise on the wide expanse of Rutland Water. The 'Rutland Belle' operates Apr, Sat-Sun, May-Sept, daily, Oct, Sat-Sun. Schools Price B.

BUS TRIPS

DERBYSHIRE

Derbys/Notts border, 0114 248 9139. A 1948 Bedford bus connects attractions on a circular route, including Bolsover Castle, Hardwick Hall, Five Pits Trail, Worksop and Creswell Crags. Various ticket options available. Telephone for Summer timetable.

Chesterfield (near), Hardwick Estate, Doe Lea, 01246 850430. A one-hour 'Behind the Scenes' tour on a 1948 Bedford bus. Explores the estate on both sides of the motorway. Telephone for Summer timetable.

LEICESTERSHIRE

Leicester, 01789 299123. During the Summer, an open-top double-decker bus connects various attractions including the Great Central Railway, National Space Centre and Abbey Park. Commentary available. Ticket valid all day.

LINCOLNSHIRE

Lincoln, 01789 299123. An open-top double-decker bus connects various attractions including Brayford Pool, the Castle and Cathedral. Commentary available. Ticket valid all day. Operates Easter-Sept.

Skegness, 07831 669556. Instead of walking along the sands, experience a ride in this 4x4 beach ferry. Operates daily during the Summer.

Sutton-on-Sea, 07762 619162. Enjoy a vintage bus trip of about two miles along the promenade to Mablethorpe, via Trusthorpe. Operates daily, Easter-early Sept. Phone for details.

NOTTINGHAMSHIRE

Nottingham, 0115 911 5005. In a seven-seater Space Cruiser, enjoy a 30-minute trip from the Castle Gatehouse, through the deer park and past many of the city's attractions. Commentary available. Operates daily, Easter-Oct, 10.30am-3.30pm.

CYCLE HIRE

There are miles of traffic-free routes around reservoirs, along old railway lines, through forests or parkland. Take your own bikes or hire from one of the following centres.

DERBYSHIRE

Ashbourne, Peak Cycle Hire, Tissington Trail, 01335 343156.
Bakewell, White Peak, 01335 348603.
Fairholmes, Peak Cycle Hire, Upper Derwent Reservoirs, 01433 651261.
Hadfield, Longdendale Trail, 01457 854672.
Hayfield, Sett Valley Trail, 01663 746222.
Middleton Top, High Peak Trail, 01629 823204.
Parsley Hay, Peak Cycle Hire, High Peak Trail, 01298 84493.
Rosliston, The National Forest, 01283 515524.
Waterhouses, Brown End Farm, Manifold Trail, 01538 308313. **Peak Cycle Hire,** 01538 308609.
Wirksworth, Carsington Water, 01629 540478.

Peak District, Peak Cycle Hire, www.peakdistrict.org. There are wonderful opportunities for family cycling in the Peak District. Peak Cycle Hire have four bases each sited alongside a different trail. Choose between Ashbourne (01335 343156) on the Tissington Trail, Parsley Hay (01298 84493) on the High Peak Trail, Waterhouses (01538 308609) on the Manifold Trail and Fairholmes (01433 651261) which gives access to the Upper Derwent Reservoirs. Each Centre has a mass of various bikes and trailers, all of which are new each year. Maps, helmets and instruction are also available. Schools **Open all year Check out page 34.**

LEICESTERSHIRE

Moira, The National Forest and Ashby Wolds Trail, 01530 415021.

LINCOLNSHIRE

Long Sutton, The Fens, 01945 440346
Spalding, The Fens, 01775 722050.
Woodhall Spa, Jubilee Park, 01526 353478.

NOTTINGHAMSHIRE

Clipstone, Sherwood Pines Forest Park, 01623 822855.
Wales Bar, Rother Valley Country Park, 0114 247 1453.
Worksop, Clumber Park, 01909 476592.

RUTLAND

Oakham (near), Rutland Water Cycling, Whitwell, www.rutlandcycling.co.uk 01780 460705. An excellent landscapped track never far from the water's edge. Cycle a short distance or the full 23-mile circuit.

TRAIN TRIPS

DERBYSHIRE

Cromford, Steeple Grange Light Railway, 01246 205542. Short track with steep gradient through beautifully overgrown quarry. A branch line of former Cromford and High Peak railway. Operates Easter-Sept, Sun and Bank Hol Mons, Sat in Jul-Aug and Dec, and for Santa Specials.

Derby, Markeaton Park Light Railway, 01623 552292. Short track through park. Operating weekends and daily, late May-Oct. Also Santa Specials. Schools.

Matlock, Peak Rail, www.peakrail.co.uk 01629 580381. This preserved standard-gauge steam railway with 4.5-mile track has stations at Rowsley, Darley Dale and Matlock. Exhibition coach, picnic area, narrow-gauge railway, Santa Specials and other event days. Open most days in Summer, some Winter weekends. Schools Birthdays Price B.

Ripley (near), Midland Railway Centre, www.midlandrailwaycentre.co.uk 01773 570140. Travel 3.5 miles of track on a standard-gauge steam train and visit the exhibition hall with over 40 steam, diesel and electric engines. See the demonstration signal box and miniature railway. Also enjoy a one-mile ride on the Golden Valley narrow-gauge railway. Telephone for details of operational days and special events. Schools Birthdays Price B.

LEICESTERSHIRE

Loughborough, Great Central Railway, www.greatcentralrailway.com 01509 230726. Enjoy a standard-gauge steam train ride along eight miles of double track. Often used in film and TV drama. There are stations at Loughborough, Quorn, Rothley and Leicester North. Visit the museum, engine sheds, and wartime air raid shelter. Special events include 'Thomas the Tank Engine' weekends and Santa Specials. Telephone for details of operational dates. Schools Birthdays **Open all year** Price C.

Shackerstone, Battlefield Line Railway, www.battlefield-line-railway.co.uk 01827 880754. Visit the museum and platform tearoom, open most weekends and Bank Hol Mons. Telephone for operating dates when a standard-gauge steam or diesel train runs through attractive countryside between Shackerstone and Shenton station. Special events.

LINCOLNSHIRE

Cleethorpes, 01472 323111. Contact the TIC for details of a land train that operates along the promenade from the shops to the Lakeside, daily, Easter-early Sept.

Cleethorpes Coast Light Railway, 01472 604657, leaving from the Lakeside with its ducks, gardens and playground. Enjoy a steam train ride out of town, following the coastal path/cycleway for just over a mile. Special events. Telephone for operational dates. Schools Birthdays **Open all year** Price A.

Ludborough (near), Lincs Wolds Railway, 01507 363881. Visit this small preservation centre which is open most weekends and Bank Hol Mons. Special events include short steam rides, wartime weekends and Santa Specials.

Mablethorpe, 01507 474939. Contact the TIC for details of the land train that operates from Quebec Road along the promenade. Also take a ride on 'Daisy May', the sand train which has been running on North Beach for over 50 years.

Scunthorpe (near), Appleby Frodingham Steam Railway, 01652 657053, A free two-hour rail tour around Corus steel works, on some 20 miles of track. A guide explains about iron and steel making and you may glimpse red-hot steel being rolled in the mills. Telephone TIC for details. Operates end May-Sept. Schools.

Skegness, 01754 764821. Contact the TIC for details of a land train that runs along the promenade daily, Easter-early Sept.

NOTTINGHAMSHIRE

Ruddington, **Nottingham Transport Heritage Centre,** www.gcrailway.co.uk 0115 940 5705. Enjoy a standard-gauge steam train ride through the Country Park. Four miles of track. See various collections including buses, diesel and steam locomotives. Also miniature railway and children's playground. Open Mar-Oct, Sun and Bank Hol Mons, 10.45am-5pm. Phone for details of special events. Schools Birthdays Price B.

RUTLAND

Cottesmore, **Rutland Railway Museum,** 01572 813203. Visit to see steam and diesel locomotives and various wagons typifying railway activities in ironstone quarrying, formerly an important local activity. Open most weekends, 11am-5pm. Some weekends it's possible to enjoy a ride on the short demonstration line. Telephone for prices and timetable.

TRAMS, TROLLEY BUSES AND ROAD TRANSPORT

DERBYSHIRE

Crich, **Crich Tramway Village,** www.tramway.co.uk 0870 758 7267. Cobbled street scene with historic buildings and unlimited rides on various trams along a one-mile route. Admire a huge collection of electric, horse-drawn and steam trams. Watch restoration work in progress. Also indoor soft play, woodland walk and playgrounds. Special events. Open 14th–22nd Feb, daily, and Mar, Sat-Sun, 10.30am-4pm; 1st Apr-31st Oct, daily, 10am-5.30pm; Nov-19th Dec, Sat-Sun, 10.30am-4pm. Schools Birthdays Price B.

LINCOLNSHIRE

Lincoln, **Lincolnshire Road and Transport Museum,** Whisby Road, North Hykeham, www.lvvs.org.uk 01522 500566. The building is absolutely packed with vehicles from yesteryear including a fire engine, buses, cars and lorries. Open May-Oct, Mon-Fri, 12noon-4pm, Sun, 10am-4pm; Nov-Apr, Suns, 1-4pm. Phone for dates and prices of special open days when there are guided tours and rides. Schools **Open all year.**

Sandtoft, **Sandtoft Transport Museum,** signposted off the M180 Jn 2, www.sandtoft.org.uk 01724 711391. See the nationally acclaimed collection of trolley buses and also many other road vehicles. Nostalgic video, miniature railways and picnic areas. Children can have a go on bus simulators and enjoy the playground. Special events include rides and visits by Santa. Phone for opening dates and prices. Schools.

TRAVEL GAMES

For every letter of the alphabet starting with A
you need to spot an object beginning with that letter
before moving on to the next letter.
You can play this individually or as a team.

Sports & Leisure

Dip into this chapter for ideas of things to do. Perhaps go to the cinema, see pantomime or a live concert on stage. Support a local sports team or go ten-pin bowling, pony trekking or tobogganing. Most Sports and Leisure Centres offer a variety of activities including special schemes during school holidays. It's important to keep the children fit and useful to burn off that surplus energy. Try swimming or, for the adventurous, an outdoor pursuit like abseiling, caving, camping or watersports. This list also includes karting, quad biking, fishing, computer fun, music and movement. No-one need ever feel bored again!

ADVENTURE ACTIVITIES

PGL Activity Holidays, www.pgl.co.uk 08700 507 507, has ten UK residential centres, offering activity holidays for 7-10, 10-13 or 13-16 year olds covering football, drama, kayaking, 'Adrenaline Adventure', 'Learner Driver' and much more. There are also 'Family Active' holidays for all the family and centres in France. Winter snow sports are available in Austria. Telephone for free brochure. **Check out page 42.**

BOWLING (TEN PIN)

DERBYSHIRE: Chesterfield: **Chesterfield Bowl** Hasland 01246 550092. Derby: **Megabowl** Foresters Leisure Pk 01332 270057. Ilkeston: **AMF Bowl** Derby Rd 0115 932 2092.
LEICESTERSHIRE: Leicester: **Hollywood Bowl** Meridian Leisure Pk 0116 263 1234, **Megabowl** St Peters La 0116 251 8885.
LINCOLNSHIRE: Boston: **Boston Bowl** Rochford Tower La 01205 359525. Cleethorpes: **Bowling** Kings Rd 01472 601006, **Wimpys Kingpin** Central Promenade 01472 603682. Grantham: **Grantham Bowl** Dysart Rd 01476 592040. Lincoln: **Lincoln Bowl** Washingborough Rd 01522 522059. Mablethorpe: High St 01507 472407. Scunthorpe: **AMF Bowl** Warren Rd 01724 864225, **Ashby Bowl** Grange La South 01724 852852. Skegness: **Pier Superbowl** 01754 761341.
NOTTINGHAMSHIRE: Mansfield: **Superbowl** Stockwell Gate 01623 462000. Nottingham: **AMF** Barker Gate 0115 950 5588, **Megabowl** Redfield Way 0115 985 0820.

CINEMAS

DERBYSHIRE: Chesterfield: **Cineworld** Alma Leisure Pk 01246 278000. Derby: **Metro** Green La 01332 340170, **Showcase** Foresters Leisure Pk 01332 270300, **UCI** Meteor Centre 01332 295010. Ilkeston: **Scala** Market Pl 0115 932 4612.
LEICESTERSHIRE: Leicester: **Odeon** Freemans Pk 0870 505 0007, **Phoenix** Newarke St 0116 255 4854, **Warner** Meridian Leisure Pk 0870 240 6020. Loughborough: **Curzon** Cattle Market 01509 212261. Melton Mowbray: **The Regal** King St 01664 562251.
LINCOLNSHIRE: Boston: **Blackfriars Centre** Spain La 01205 363108, **Regal** West St 01205 350553. Grantham: **Paragon** Saint Catherines Rd 01476 570046. Grimsby: **Odeon** Freeman St 0870 505 0007. Lincoln: **Odeon** Valentine Rd 0870 505 0007. Louth: **Playhouse** Cannon St 01507 603333. Mablethorpe: **Loewen** Quebec Rd 01507 477040. Scunthorpe: **Screen** 01724 277744. Skegness: **The Tower** Lumley Rd 01754 763938. Spalding: **South Holland Centre** 01775 725031. Stamford: **Arts Centre** St Mary's St 01780 763203. Woodhall Spa: **Kinema-in-the-Woods** 01526 352166.
NOTTINGHAMSHIRE: Hucknall: **Cineplex** High St 0115 963 6377. Mansfield: **Odeon** Nottingham Rd 0870 505 0007. Newark: **Palace Theatre** Appleton Gate 01636 655755. Nottingham: **Broadway** Broad St 0115 952 6611, **Savoy** Derby Rd 0115 947 2580, **Showcase** Redfield Way 0115 986 6766. Worksop: **The Regal** Carlton Rd 01909 482896.

CLIMBING WALLS

DERBYSHIRE: Glossop: **The Leisure Centre** 01457 863223. Wirksworth: **The Leisure Centre** 01629 824717.
LEICESTERSHIRE: Leicester: **The Tower Climbing Centre** Leicester Leys 0116 233 3074.
NOTTINGHAMSHIRE: Nottingham: **The Climbing Centre** Haydn Rd 0115 924 5388.
RUTLAND: Oakham: **Rock Blok** Whitwell Rutland Water (outdoor) 01780 460060.

COMPUTER FUN

LEICESTERSHIRE: Spaceship computer suites in various venues invite group visits from nursery and primary schools. Also other community events. Contact Marie Wartley 0116 272 9100.

CRAFT ACTIVITIES

DERBYSHIRE: Ashbourne (near): **Fizzpotzz Parties** by The Village Soap Company, Fenny Bentley www.villagesoapco.co.uk 01335 350195. Book a party leader to run a birthday party in your own home (or a venue near Ashbourne) and enjoy a great range of 'make your own' activities including making lip balm, soap, bath bombs, shampoo and bubble bath. Parties last a couple of hours. All professional cosmetic ingredients are included. Birthdays **Check out page 42.**

CRAZY GOLF

DERBYSHIRE: Buxton: Pavilion Gardens. Derby: Mundy Play Centre Markeaton Pk 01332 343075. Glossop: Manor Park. Rosliston: Forestry Centre 01283 563483. Swadlincote: Eureka Park.
LEICESTERSHIRE: Blaby: Lutterworth Rd 0116 278 4804. Market Bosworth: Bosworth Water Trust 01455 291876.
LINCOLNSHIRE: Chapel Saint Leonards: South Rd. Cleethorpes: Alexandra Rd 01472 697734. Mablethorpe: Dunes Gardens, North Promenade, Queens Park. Skegness: Tower Esplanade 01754 612575. Sutton-on-Sea: Pleasure Gardens.
NOTTINGHAMSHIRE: Retford: Kings Park. Worksop: Memorial Gardens.

FISHING

A 108-page Midlands Regional Fishing Guide is free and produced by the local Environment Agency. It lists places to fish. 0906 300 3344.

GOLF

This selection of child-friendly venues includes local putting greens and various pitch and putt courses. Further centres can be found in Yellow Pages.
DERBYSHIRE: Buxton: Fairfield Common 01298 74444. Derby: Chaddesdon Park 01332 367800, Markeaton Park 01332 384494. Ilkeston: Rutland Recreation Ground West End Dri. Matlock: Hall Leys Park.
LEICESTERSHIRE: Breedon-on-the-Hill: Priory Nurseries 01332 862406. Coalville: Snibston Discovery Park Golf Link 01530 811622. Hinkley: Holycroft Park. Leicester: Humberstone Heights 0116 299 5570, Lutterworth Rd Blaby 0116 278 4804. Loughborough: Poplar Rd 01509 267766. Market Harborough: Welland Park. Melton Mowbray: Ashfordby Rd 01664 567846.
LINCOLNSHIRE: Boston: Hubberts Bridge 01205 290670. Gainsborough: Mill Field Laughterton 01427 718473. Grantham: Carlton Scroop 01400 250796. Lincoln: Thorpe-on-the-Hill 01522 680159, Washingborough Rd 01522 522059. Newark: Newark Golf Centre

Here's a fun music programme that can benefit your children, your community and you!

Rhythm Time introduces babies and pre-school children to music. It's a great boost to every child's development and confidence. These *quality music classes* have already benefited thousands of children all over the country.

Call *Rhythm Time* Head Office 0121 711 4224 or visit our website to see if there is one of our fun classes in your area.

Exciting opportunities

We are looking for enthusiastic people to run *Rhythm Time* classes as their own franchise. A good singing voice is the only essential requirement. Teaching experience is beneficial but not essential, since in depth training is given by a music teacher.

If you are interested in this wonderful opportunity call *Rhythm Time* Head Office on 0121 711 4224

Rhythm Time

EARLY LEARNING THROUGH MUSIC

www.rtfg.co.uk

For more information call 0121 711 4224

01636 702161. Scunthorpe: Messingham 01724 762945. Skegness: South Parade Pitch and Putt. Stamford: Recreation Park.
NOTTINGHAMSHIRE: Long Eaton: West Park. Nottingham: Bulwell Forest 0115 976 3172, Woodthorpe Grange 0115 915 2729, University Park. Retford: Kings Park. Southwell: Norwood Park 01636 816626. Worksop: Memorial Gardens, Whitwell 01909 723608

ICE SKATING

LINCOLNSHIRE: Grimsby: **Grimsby Leisure Centre** 01472 323100.
NOTTINGHAMSHIRE: Nottingham: **National Ice Centre** www.nottingham-arena.com 0115 853 3000.

KARTING

DERBYSHIRE: Buxton: Harpor Hill 01298 71037. Chesterfield: Pottery La East (indoor track) 01246 551116. Elvaston: 01332 751938.
LEICESTERSHIRE: Great Stretton: Gartree Rd 0116 259 2900. Thurmaston: Humberstone La (indoor track) 0116 269 7878. Upper Broughton: 01664 822750.
LINCOLNSHIRE: Ancaster: Pit Hill Farm 01400 230306. Caythorpe (near): 01636 626424. Grimsby: Chequered Flag 01472 823823. Tattershall: Lodge Rd 01526 344566.
NOTTINGHAMSHIRE: Langar: Airfield Site 01949 861155. Newark: Elk Winthorpe Airfield 01636 673322. Rufford: Amen Corner 01623 822205.

MUSIC AND MOVEMENT

Jo Jingles, www.jojingles.co.uk 01494 719360, is a leading music and singing experience with an educational slant for children aged 6 months to 7 years. Exciting and stimulating classes run at venues all over the country. For details on classes in your area or for information on the franchise opportunity please call 01494 719360, email: headoffice@jojingles.co.uk or visit the website. Birthdays **Check out page 42.**

Monkey Music, www.monkeymusic.co.uk 01582 766464, runs music classes for babies and children aged between 6 months and 4 years at venues all over the UK. Business franchise opportunities are available in this area. Please telephone for details. **Check out page 52.**

Rhythm Time, www.rtfg.co.uk 0121 711 4224, runs quality music classes for babies, toddlers and older children. Interesting new ideas and songs to help development and musical skills. Courses written by a music teacher. Classes opening all over the UK. For details or information about the exciting franchise opportunity please call or email kathy@rtfg.co.uk. **Check out page 44.**

Singing Sally's, www.singtogether.co.uk 0116 255 5665, is a club for children under 5, based around song and rhyme. Please call for details and **check out page 46.**

OUTDOOR PURSUITS

Activities may include hill walking, rock climbing, mine exploration, survival skills, abseiling, potholing, archery, canoeing, team building, orienteering, caving and camping. Some places take schools and youth clubs, others family groups. Some run a programme, others design a course on request. Several offer residential facilities and there is even an aerial assault course!

DERBYSHIRE: Buxton: **Dave Edwards Activities** www.dave-edwardsandassociates.net 01298 85375, **Escape** www.escape-uk.com 07000 437 2273, **White Hall Outdoor Education Centre** www.whitehallcentre.co.uk 01298 23260. Castleton: **Hollowford Centre** www.hollowford.org.uk 01433 620377. Crich: **Lea Green Education Centre** 01629 534561. Cromford: **Challenge the Peak** www.challengethepeak.com 01709 328828. Darley Dale: **David Matthews Activities** www.dm-adventure.supanet.com 01629 732445, **Derwent**

Outdoor Pursuits www.derwent-pursuits.co.uk 01629 824511. Edale: **The Peak Centre** www.the-peak-centre.org.uk 01433 670254, **YHA Activity Centre** www.yha.org.uk 01433 670302. Longshaw: **Parson House Outdoor Pursuits Centre** 01433 631017. Midway: **Pennine Outdoor Pursuits** 01283 210666. Pleasley Vale: **Outdoor Pursuits Centre** 01623 812530.
LEICESTERSHIRE: Leicester: **Outdoor Pursuits Centre** 0116 268 1426. Quorn: **Beaumanor Park Outdoor Education Centre** 01509 890119.
NOTTINGHAMSHIRE: Clipstone: **Go Ape** Sherwood Pines Forest Park (aerial assault course) www.goape.cc 0870 444 5562. Farnsfield: **Lockwell Hill Activity Centre** 01623 883067. Newark: **Walesby Forest Activity Centre** 01623 860202. Sutton-in-Ashfield: **The Mill Adventure Base** 01623 556110. Worksop: **Sandhills Centre** 01909 501325.

TRAVEL GAMES

Each choose a letter.

See how many objects you can spot, either in the car or out of the window, beginning with the letter in a given time.

Keep a list.

QUAD BIKING

LEICESTERSHIRE: Leicester: **Outdoor Pursuits Centre** 0116 268 1426.
LINCOLNSHIRE: Brigg: **Newstead Priory** 01652 653283.
NOTTINGHAMSHIRE: Farnsfield: **Lockwell Activity Centre** 01623 883067. Langar: Airfield site 01949 861155. Nottingham: Holme Pierrepont 0115 921 2584.

SKIING, SNOWBOARDING AND TOBOGGANING

Tamworth (just over the border into Staffordshire): **SnowDome,** Leisure Island, River Drive, www.snowdome.co.uk 08705 000011, offers a wide range of unique and fun activities for children and adults of all ages to enjoy. Everyone can get involved and have a great time on the new ice skating rink and real snow slopes. It's the perfect venue for a family outing. You can try out tobogganing, sledging, skiing, snowboarding and even the latest fun, snow tubing! This involves speeding and spinning down the slope in specially designed inflatable tubes. There is Adrenalin Tubing for over 12s and adults, Junior Tubing for 7-12s and Tiny Tubing for 3-7s! Or enjoy racing your family and friends in your very own steerable toboggan. Children must be over 1m tall and under 10s must be accompanied by an adult. Children aged 3-7 can enjoy sledging sessions in the Snow Academy, a separate nursery slope. Pre-booking is advisable. Open daily, 9am-11pm, please telephone for slope timetables. **Open all year** Price E **Check out page 46.**

DERBYSHIRE: Swadlincote: **Swadlincote Ski and Snowboard Centre,** Hill St, www.jnll.co.uk 01283 217200, offers great fun for all the family. It has a 160m dry ski slope, separate nursery slope and an exhilarating toboggan run winding its way down 650m, the only one of its kind in the Midlands. Enjoy yourselves throughout the evening, as the hill is well floodlit. High standards of ski and snowboard tuition are available for all levels and there are club meetings, with race programmes and competitions. Resturant and gift shop. Open daily, 10am-10pm. Schools Birthdays **Check out page 46.**

DERBYSHIRE: Swadlincote: **Ski and Snowboard Centre** 01283 217200.
LINCOLNSHIRE: Stamford: Tallington Lakes 01778 346342.

DERBYSHIRE: Derby: **County Cricket Ground** 01332 383211, **Derby County Football Ground** Pride Pk 01332 202202.

LEICESTERSHIRE: Castle Donington: **Donington Park** (motor racing) 01332 810048. Earl Shilton: **Mallory Park** (motor racing) 01455 842931. Leicester: **Leicester City Football** Walkers Stadium 0870 040 6000, **Leicester County Cricket Ground** Grace Rd 0116 283 2128, **Leicester Tigers Rugby** Welford Rd 0116 254 1607. Loughborough: **University International Athletics** 01509 263171.

LINCOLNSHIRE: Lincoln: **County Cricket Ground** 01522 688008. Louth (near): **Cadwell Park** (motor racing) 01507 343248.

NOTTINGHAMSHIRE: Nottingham: **National Ice Centre** 0115 853 3000, **National Watersports Centre** Holme Pierrepont 0115 982 1212, **Nottingham Forest Football** The City Ground 0115 982 4453, **Nottingham Tennis Centre** University Boulevard 0115 915 0000, **Notts County Cricket Ground** Trent Bridge 0115 982 3000, **Notts County Football** 0115 952 9000.

Abbreviations: LC: Leisure Centre, SC: Sports Centre. * centre has a swimming pool.

DERBYSHIRE: Alfreton: **Alfreton LC*** Church St 01773 834817. Ashbourne: **Ashbourne LC*** Station Rd 01335 343712. Belper: **Belper LC*** Kilbourne Rd 01773 825285. Chesterfield: **Queens Park SC*** Boythorpe Rd 01246 345555. Clay Cross: **Sharpley Park LC*** Market St 01246 862461. Clowne: **Clowne SC** Mansfield Rd 01246 810902. Derby: **Derby College SC** Mackworth 01332 520371, **Lancaster SC** Chapel St 01332 361549, **Moorways SC*** Moor La 01332 363686, **Queens LC*** Cathedral Rd 01332 716620, **Shaftesbury SC** Shaftesbury Cresc 01332 255603, **Springwood LC** Oakwood 01332 664433, **Willows SC** Willow Row 01332 204004. Dronfield: **Dronfield SC*** Civic Centre 01246 416166. Etwall: **Etwall LC*** 01283 733348. Glapwell: **Glapwell SC** The Green 01623 810979. Glossop: **Glossop LC** High St East 01457 863223. Heanor: **Heanor LC*** Hands Rd 01773 769711. Ilkeston: **Albion LC** East St 0115 944 0200. Loscoe: **Charles Hill SC** Flamstead Ave 01773 761551. Matlock: **Sherwood Hall LC** Lime Tree Rd 01629 56111. Measham: **Measham LC** High St 01530 274061. Melbourne: **Melbourne LC** High St 01332 863522. New Mills: **New Mills LC*** Hyde Bank Rd 01663 745424. Ripley: **Ripley LC*** Derby Rd 01773 746531. Selston: **Selston LC** Chapel Rd 01773 781800. Shirebrook: **Kissingate LC** Park Rd 01623 748313. Staveley: **Middlecroft LC*** Calver St 01246 345666. Swadlincote: **Swadlincote LC*** Green Bank 01283 216269. Wirksworth: **Wirksworth LC*** Water La 01629 824717.

LEICESTERSHIRE: Ashby-de-la-Zouch: **Hood Park LC*** North St 01530 412181. Fleckney: **Fleckney LC** Recreation Rd 0116 240 3755. Hinkley: **Hinkley LC*** Coventry Rd 01455 610011. Kibworth Beauchamp: **Kibworth Beauchamp SC** Smeeton Rd 0116 279 6971. Leicester: **Aylestone LC*** 2 Knighton La East 0116 233 3040, **Cossington Street SC*** 0116 233 3060, **Enderby LC*** Mill La 0116 275 0234, **Guthlaxton College Sports Hall** Station Rd Wigston 0116 281 2991, **Huncote LC** Sportsfield La 0116 275 0246, **Leicester Leys LC*** Beaumont Way 0116 233 3070, **New Park LC*** St Oswalds Rd 0116 233 3080, **Parklands SC** Wigston Rd Oadby 0116 272 0789, **Southfields Drive SC** 0116 283 9047, **Spence Street SC** 0116 299 5584. Loughborough: **Burleigh Community College SC*** 01509 554400, **Charnwood LC*** Browns La 01509 611080. Market Harborough: **Market Harborough LC*** Northampton Rd 01858 410115. Melton Mowbray: **Melton Mowbray LC** Ashfordby Rd 01664 851111. Thurmaston: **Elizabeth Park SC** Checkland Rd 0116 260 2519. Whitwick: **Hermitage LC*** Silver St 01530 811215.

LINCOLNSHIRE: Barton-on-Humber: **Barton SC** Newport St 01652 660016, **Baysgarth LC*** Brigg Rd 01652 632511. Brigg: **Ancholme LC*** Scawby Rd 01652 652031. Bourne: **Bourne LC*** Queens Rd 01778 421435. Boston: **Kirton LC** Willington Rd 01205 724099. Caistor: **Caistor SC** Grimsby Rd 01472 852404. Cleethorpes: **Cleethorpes LC*** Kingsway 01472 313200. Epworth: **Epworth LC** Burnham Rd 01427 873845. Gainsborough: **West**

Lindsey LC* The Avenue 01427 615169. Grantham: **Grantham Meres LC** Trent Rd 01476 581930. Grimsby: **Clee Fields SC** Ladysmith Rd 01472 351913, **Grimsby LC** Cromwell Rd 01472 323100, **King George V Athletics Stadium** 01472 323228. Immingham: **Immingham SC** Washdyke La 01469 516001. Lincoln: **Birchwoods LC** Birchwood Ave 01522 873696, **North Kesteven LC*** Moor La North Hykeham 01522 883311, **Yarborough LC*** Riseholme Rd 01522 873600. Mablethorpe: **Mablethorpe LC*** Station Rd 01507 472129. Market Deeping: **Deepings LC*** Park Rd 01778 344072. Market Rasen: **De Aston SC** Legsby Rd 01673 842695. Scunthorpe: **Bottesford SC** Ontario Rd 01724 282146, **Scunthorpe LC** Carlton St 01724 280555. Skegness: **Earl of Scarborough LC** Burgh Rd 01754 610352. Sleaford: **Northgate Sports Hall** Millfield Tce 01529 303004, **Sleaford LC** East Banks 01529 303081. Spalding: **Castle SC** Albion St 01775 710496. Stamford: **Stamford LC*** Drift Rd 01780 765522.

NOTTINGHAMSHIRE: Bingham: **Bingham LC*** The Banks 01949 838628. Bircotes: **Bircotes LC*** Whitehouse Rd 01302 743979. Calverton: **Calverton LC*** Flates La 0115 965 3781. Cotgrave: **Cotgrave LC*** Woodview 0115 989 2916. Creswell: **Creswell LC*** Duke St 01909 721371. Dronfield: **Dronfield SC** High St 01246 416166. East Leake: **East Leake LC*** Lantern La 01509 852956. Hucknall: **Edgewood LC** Christchurch Rd 0115 956 8790, **Hucknall LC*** Linby Rd 0115 956 8750. Huthwaite: **Huthwaite LC** New St 01623 457130. Keyworth: **Keyworth LC*** Church Dri 0115 937 5582. Killamarsh: **Killamarsh SC** Sheffield Rd 0114 248 5554. Kimberley: **Kimberley LC*** Newdigate St 0115 917 3366. Kirby-in-Ashfield: **Festival Hall LC** Hodgkinson Rd 01623 457100. Long Eaton: **West Park LC*** Wilsthorpe Rd 0115 946 1400. Mansfield: **Water Meadows LC** Bath St 01623 463880. Mansfield Woodhouse: **Manor Park SC** Kingsley Ave 01623 425116. Newark: **Grove LC*** London Rd 01636 655780. New Ollerton: **Dukeries LC*** Whinney La 01623 862469. Nottingham: **Arnold LC*** High St 0115 956 0733, **Bramcote LC*** Derby Rd 0115 917 3000, **Carlton Forum LC*** Conningsworth Rd 0115 987 2333, **Chilwell Olympic** Beeston 0115 917 3333, **Clifton LC*** Southchurch Dri 0115 915 2333, **Friesland SC** Sandiacre 0115 949 0400, **Harvey Haddon SC** Bilborough 0115 915 1515, **John Carroll LC*** Denman St Radford 0115 915 1535, **Lenton LC*** Willoughby St 0115 915 0095, **Noel Street LC*** New Basford 0115 915 1545, **Portland LC*** Muskham St The Meadows 0115 915 0015, **Southglade LC*** Southglade Rd Bestwood 0115 915 1525, **Tennis Centre** University Boulevard 0115 915 0000, **Victoria LC*** Gedling St Sneiton 0115 915 5600. Rainworth: **Rainworth LC*** Warsop La 01623 466266. Ravenshead: **Ravenshead LC** Longdale La 01623 491522. Retford: **Retford LC*** West Carr Rd 01777 706509. Selston: **Selston LC** Chapel Rd 01773 781800. Southwell: **Southwell LC*** Nottingham Rd 01636 813000. Sutton-in-Ashfield: **Sutton-in-Ashfield LC** High Pavement 01623 457666. Warsop: **Meden SC*** Burns La 01623 842865. West Bridgford: **Rushcliffe Arena** Rugby Rd 0115 981 4027, **Rushcliffe LC*** Boundary Rd 0115 923 4921. Worksop: **Worksop LC*** Valley Rd 01909 473937, **Bassetlaw LC** Eastgate 01909 480164.

SWIMMING POOLS (INDOOR)

Check out listing of Sports & Leisure Centres above. Those marked with * have a pool.
DERBYSHIRE: Buxton: St Johns Rd 01298 26548. Derby: **Moorways** Moor La 01332 341736. Eckington: Gosber St 01246 433071. Glossop: Dinting Rd 01457 863128. Illkeston: Victoria Pk 0115 944 0400. Matlock: Imperial Rd 01629 582843.
LEICESTERSHIRE: Birstall: **Birstall Swimming Pool** Stonehill Ave 0116 267 3461. Countesthorpe: **GDL Pools** Bassett Ave 0116 233 7326. Desford: **Bosworth Community College** Leicester La 01455 822841. Leicester: Downing Dri Evington 0116 299 5575, **St Margarets Baths** Vaughan Way 0116 233 3090. Loughborough: **Loughborough University Pool** Epinal Way 01509 226200. Lutterworth: Bitteswell Rd 01455 552477. Melton Mowbray: **Waterfield Leisure Pools** Dalby Rd 01664 563550. Quorn: **Rawlins Community College** Loughborough Rd 01509 622822. Shepshed: **Hind Leys Community College** Forest Rd 01509 504511. Syston: **South Charnwood Swimming Pool** Parkstone Rd 0116 264 0057. Wigston: Station Rd 0116 288 1758.

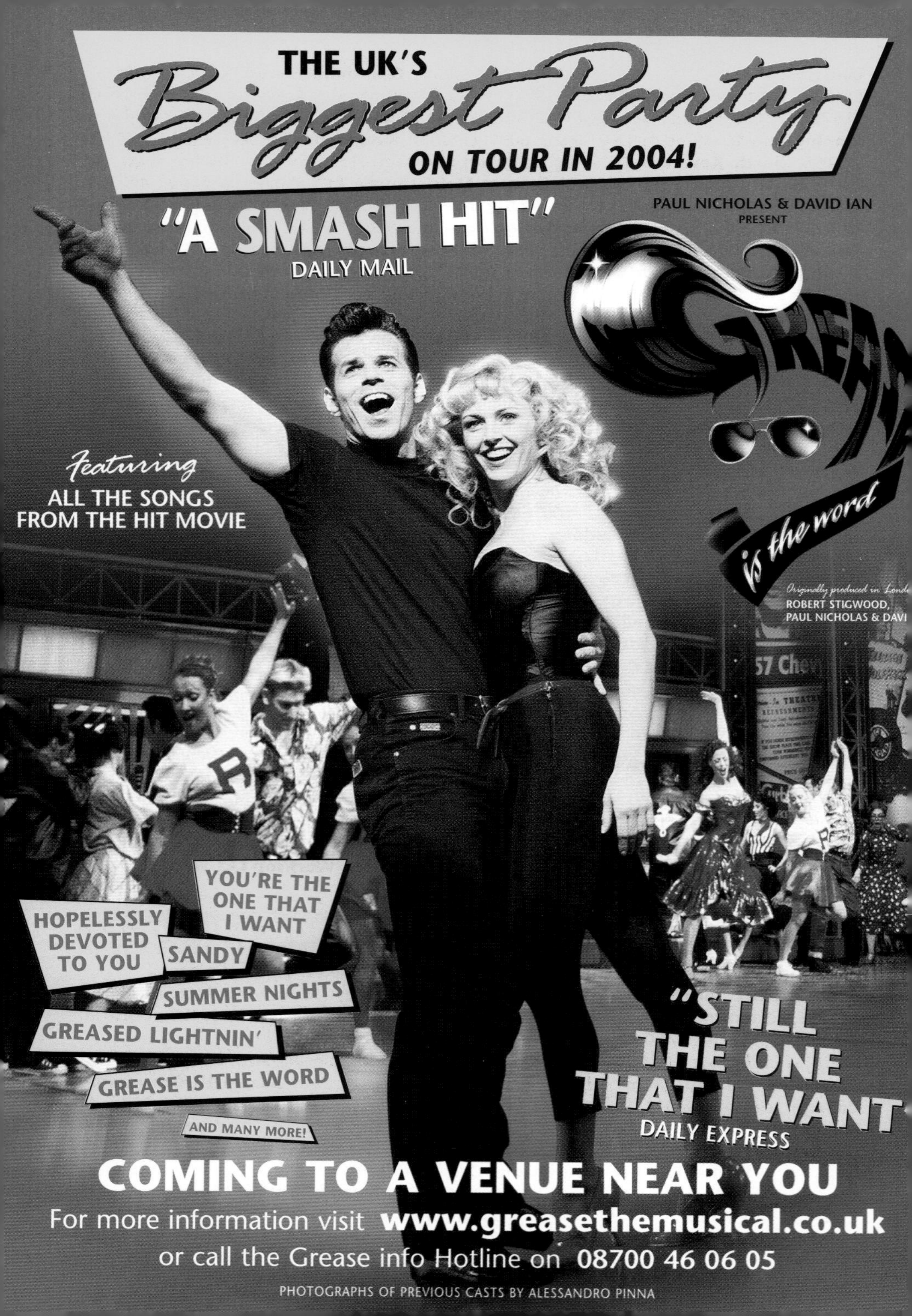
THE UK'S
Biggest Party
ON TOUR IN 2004!
"A SMASH HIT"
DAILY MAIL
PAUL NICHOLAS & DAVID IAN
PRESENT
is the word
Originally produced in Londo
ROBERT STIGWOOD,
PAUL NICHOLAS & DAVI
Featuring
ALL THE SONGS
FROM THE HIT MOVIE
HOPELESSLY DEVOTED TO YOU
YOU'RE THE ONE THAT I WANT
SANDY
SUMMER NIGHTS
GREASED LIGHTNIN'
GREASE IS THE WORD
AND MANY MORE!
"STILL THE ONE THAT I WANT"
DAILY EXPRESS
COMING TO A VENUE NEAR YOU
For more information visit www.greasethemusical.co.uk
or call the Grease info Hotline on 08700 46 06 05
PHOTOGRAPHS OF PREVIOUS CASTS BY ALESSANDRO PINNA

LINCOLNSHIRE: Boston: **Geoff Moulder Pools** Rowley Rd 01205 363483. Epworth: Burnham Rd 01427 875493. Grimsby: Scarthoe Rd 01472 323500. Horncastle: Coronation Walk 01507 522489. Immingham: Princes St 01469 516003. Louth: Riverhead Rd 01507 604738. Scunthorpe: **Riddings Pool** Enderby Rd 01724 280666. Skegness: Grand Parade 01754 610675. Spalding: Pinchbeck Rd 01775 725978.

NOTTINGHAMSHIRE: Edwinstowe: **South Forest** Clipstone Rd 01623 823866. Mansfield: **Sherwood Baths** Westdale Rd 01623 463082. Nottingham: **Beechdale Swimming Centre** Bilborough 0115 915 1575, **Elliot Durham Pool** Ransom Rd St Anns 0115 915 0055, Ken Martin Hucknall Rd 0115 915 1555. Ratcliffe-on-Trent: Cropwell Rd 0115 933 24880. Sutton-in-Ashfield: Brook St 01623 457089.

RUTLAND: Oakham: **Vale of Catmose Community College** Cold Overton Rd 01572 722286.

SWIMMING POOLS (OUTDOOR)

DERYSHIRE: Hathersage: Old Fellows Rd 01433 650843.
LEICESTERSHIRE: Ashby-de-la-Zouch: **Hood Park Leisure Centre** 01530 412181.
LINCOLNSHIRE: Bourne: Abbey Lawns. Grantham: Dysart Park. Skegness: Grand Parade 01754 610675. Woodhall Spa: Jubilee Park 01526 353478.
NOTTINGHAMSHIRE: Nottingham: **Ken Martin Swimming Pool** Hucknall Rd 0115 915 1555.

THEATRES & CONCERT VENUES

Grease on Tour, www.greasethemusical.co.uk   Grease the Musical is on tour throughout the country this year and is going to be at a theatre near you! The show is packed with explosive energy, vibrant 1950s pop culture and lots of unforgettable songs. Take the family to this fabulous Rock'n'Roll musical filled with irresistible groovy and memorable moments. Don't miss it! For full information, casting details, competitions, special offers and full tour venues and dates log on to the website above. **Check out page 50.**

DERBYSHIRE: Buxton: **Opera House** 01298 72190. Chesterfield: **Arts Centre** 01246 500578, **Pomegranate** 01246 345222, **Winding Wheel** 01246 345333. Derby: **Assembly Rooms and Guildhall Theatre** 01322 255800, **The Playhouse** 01332 363275.
LEICESTERSHIRE: Coalville: **Century Theatre** Snibston 01530 813608. Hinckley: **Concordia Theatre** 01455 615005. Leicester: **De Montfort Hall** 0116 233 3111, **The Little Theatre** 0116 255 1302, **Phoenix Arts Centre** 0116 255 4854. Loughborough: **Charnwood Theatre** 01509 231914. Market Harborough: **Church Square Theatre** 01858 463673.
LINCOLNSHIRE: Boston: **Blackfriars Arts Centre** 01205 363108. Gainsborough: **Trinity Arts Centre** 01427 676655. Grantham: **Guildhall Arts Centre** 01476 406158. Grimsby: **Caxton Theatre** 01472 345167, **Grimsby Auditorium** 01472 311311. Lincoln: **Theatre Royal** 01522 534570. Louth: **Riverhead Theatre** 01507 600350. Mablethorpe: **Dunes Family Entertainment Centre** 01507 479999. Scunthorpe: **Plowright Theatre** 01724 2777333. Skegness: **Embassy Centre** 01754 768333. Spalding: **South Holland Centre** 01775 725031. Spilsby: **Spilsby Theatre** 01790 752936. Stamford: **The Arts Centre** 01780 763203.
NOTTINGHAMSHIRE: Averham: **Robin Hood Theatre** 01636 812291. Kirby in Ashfield: **Festival Hall** 01623 457101. Long Eaton: **Duchess Theatre** 0115 972 9195. Mansfield: **Palace Theatre** 0845 658 4458. Newark: **Palace Theatre** 01636 655755. Nottingham: **The Arts Theatre** 0115 947 6096, **Lace Market Theatre** 0115 950 7201, **Nottingham Arena** 0115 853 3000, **Playhouse** 0115 941 9419, **Royal Concert Hall and Theatre Royal** 0115 989 5555. Retford: **Little Theatre** 01777 702002, **Majestic Theatre** 01777 706866. Worksop: **The Regal Centre** 01909 482896.
RUTLAND: Little Castleton: **Tolethorpe Hall Open Air Theatre** 01780 754381. Oakham: **Queen Elizabeth Theatre** 01572 758654.

Abbreviations: B: Bellboating, C: Canoeing, JS: Jet Skiing, K: Kayaking, RBd: Raft Building, S: Sailing, SDv: Scuba Diving, W: Windsurfing, WS: Water Skiing, WWR:White Water Rafting.

DERBYSHIRE: Cromford: **Derwent Outdoor Pursuits** 01629 824511 C. Derby: **Pennine Canoe Centre** 01283 210666 C. Edale: **YHA Activity Centre** 01433 670302 C K RBd. Wirksworth: **Carsington Reservoir** 01629 540478 C K RBd S W.

LEICESTERSHIRE: Leicester: **Outdoor Pursuit Centre** 0116 268 1426 B C K. Market Bosworth: **Bosworth Water Trust** 01455 291876 C S W. Quorn: **Beaumanor Park Outdoor Education Centre** 01509 890119 C. Sapcote: **Stoney Cove** 01455 272768 SDv.

LINCOLNSHIRE: Ingoldmells: **Water Leisure Park** 01754 820555 WS. Lincoln: **Sceptre Subaqua** 01522 803656 SDv, Thorpe-on-the-Hill 01522 501357 WS. Louth: **Covenham Watersports** 01507 363709 C S WS. Stamford: Tallington Lakes 01778 347000 C JS S WWS.

NOTTINGHAMSHIRE: Long Eaton: Church Wilne 01332 875574 JS WS. Nottingham: **Lakeside Adventure Base** Holme Pierrepont 0115 982 5755 C K S WS WWR, **National Watersports Centre** Holme Pierrepont 0115 982 1212 C K S WS WWR. Sutton-in-Ashfield: **Kings Mill Adventure Base** 01623 556110 C S. Wales Bar: Rother Valley Country Park 0114 247 1453 C S W WS. Worksop: **Sandhills Lake Adventure Base** 01909 501325 C K S.

RUTLAND: Oakham: **Anglian Watersports Centre** Rutland Water 01780 460154 CK RBdSW.

Introduce children to Youth Hostels for years of enjoyable family holidays! There are over 200 Youth Hostels in England and Wales based in towns, cities, on the coast or in the countryside and most have family rooms. You can self-cater or be cooked for, stay for one night or as long as you like; youth hostelling offers flexibility and choice. New for 2004 is the 'Top Bunk Club', especially for children aged 5-12 years. To find out more visit www.yha.org.uk or call 0870 770 8868 and quote 'Let's Go 04'. For details of 25% off membership offer **check out advert below.**

Farms, Wildlife & Nature Parks

Most children love animals. In the East Midlands there's a wide variety, from traditional farm favourites to the more exotic; there are even lions, elephants and alligators. Learn about conservation and ecology and explore woodland, beautiful gardens, heath and wetland. Go on a hunt for mini-beasts, join a fungus foray, plant a tree or marvel at butterflies. In this chapter you are spoilt for choice.

The places listed here have admission charges, but there are places of natural interest which are free to visit. Check out the 'Free Places' chapter as well so you don't miss anything.

DERBYSHIRE

Extensive throughout mid and north Derbyshire:
Peak District National Park, www.peakdistrict.org 01629 816200, covers hundreds of square miles and has wonderful scenery with abundant wildlife. In 1951, it was the first area in the UK to be designated a National Park, and is now the second most visited National Park in the world. White Peak has deep valleys and green pastures criss-crossed by dry stone walls. Dark Peak to the north, is a harsher, wilder area with gritstone crags and grouse moorland.
National Park Rangers visit schools, organise playschemes, lead guided walks and nature discovery days. The National Trust manages 12% of the Peak Park and has an annual programme of wildlife events, many with children's activities. Details from High Peak Estate Office 01433 670368, South Peak Estate Office 01335 350503, Longshaw Estate Office 01433 631757.

Bakewell (near), Chatsworth Farmyard and Adventure Playground,
www.chatsworth.org 01246 582204. Adjacent to the house, this collection of farm animals includes a shire horse, sheep, cows and pigs. Watch the milking demonstration and enjoy an excellent adventure playground. Open 17th Mar–19th Dec, daily, 10.30am-5.30pm. Schools Birthdays **Price B.**

Castleton, Losehill Hall, www.peakdistrict.org 01433 620373. Day and residential opportunities for schools. Environmental/wildlife education with fieldwork in a variety of locations. Visits Manager Liz Ballard. Schools **Open all year.**

Chapel-en-le-Frith (near), Chestnut Centre, www.ottersandowls.co.uk 01298 814099. One-mile nature trail through field and woodlands. Display boards and various enclosures with otters, owls, wildcats, foxes and deer. Conservation club for 4-11 year olds. Open daily, (weekends only in Jan), 10.30am-5.30pm (dusk in Winter). Schools Birthdays **Open all year Price B.**

Crich (near), Lea Green Education Centre, 01629 534561. A large historic mansion, set in fine parkland. Day and residential opportunities in environmental and wildlife education. Schools **Open all year.**
Lea Gardens, 01629 534380. On the hillside with steep twisting paths. Take a stroll through woodland gardens with excellent rhododendrons and azaleas. Open daily, Mar-Jun, 10am-5pm. **Price A.**

Etwall (near), Highfields Farm, Heage Lane, off A516 Derby-Hilton road, www.highfieldshappyhens.co.uk 01283 730980. Visit the farm shop and walk around the paddocks to see sheep and cows. This is a free-range egg farm with 20,000 hens, at least one shed is always open. Phone for details of special events.

Hartington (near), Lower Hurst Farm, 01298 84900. This organic farm is open the first Friday every month to sell produce and allow visitors to see cattle and follow a farm trail by the attractive River Dove. Phone for details of additional public open days when there are guided trailer tours.

Kettleshulme (near), Dunge Valley Gardens, 01663 733787. Remote and beautifully situated in the rolling Pennine Hills. Explore little paths through rhododendrons and across streams. Visit the tearoom or perhaps walk over moorland to Windgather Rocks. Open Apr-Aug, phone for details. Price A.

Matlock (near), Matlock Farm Park, 01246 590200. Follow the path between paddocks to see various animals including llamas, cattle and goats. Small animals may be available to cuddle or help feed. Mini go-karts, pre-booked pony rides and picnic area. Open Easter–end Oct, daily, 10am-4.30pm, Nov-mid Dec, Sat-Sun, 10am-4pm. Schools Birthdays Price B.
Red House Stables and Carriage Museum, Darley Dale, 01629 733583. Visit to admire the horses but also see various carriages used in film and TV. Pre-booked pony rides, event days and visits by Santa. Phone for prices. Open daily, 10am-5pm (4pm Winter). Schools Birthdays **Open all year.**

Matlock Bath, Aquarium and Hologram Gallery, North Parade, 01629 583624. See various fish and buy food to feed the giant Koi carp in an open-air roof-top pool. Also, a collection of gemstones and hologram pictures. Open daily, Easter-Oct, 10am-5.30pm. Schools Price A.

Netherseal (near), Grange Wood Zoo, www.safari-parties.co.uk 01283 760541. This mini-zoo has exotic rainforest animals, birds, reptiles and insects. Learn about ring-tailed lemurs, the fascinating iguanas and meet 'Dougie' the magnificent toucan. Phone for details of 'Safari Parties' and public open days. Schools Birthdays **Open all year.**

Rosliston, Beehive Farm Centre, 01283 761467. Newly planted with trees, this site has lakes and meadows. Try fishing or follow one of the waymarked paths. Playground and small farm animals. Breakfast and other refreshments served. Open Summer, Wed-Sun, 8.30am-4pm; Winter, Wed-Fri, 8.30am-2.30pm, Sat-Sun, 8.30am-4pm. Birthdays **Open all year** Price A.

Rowsley, Wind in the Willows, www.windinthewillows.info 01629 733433. An indoor attraction with video and various tableaux with characters from this famous story. Little children can sit in Toad's caravan! Find out about real moles, voles, toads and badgers in 'Wide World'. Open daily, 10am-5.30pm (4pm Winter). Schools Birthdays **Open all year** Price B.

LEICESTERSHIRE

Extensive in NW Leicestershire and neighbouring counties:
The National Forest, www.nationalforest.org 01283 551211, covers 200 square miles and includes parts of Leicestershire, Staffordshire and Derbyshire. The long-term aim of this massive programme of regeneration is for a third of the area to be wooded, a goal which includes planting 30 million trees. Ranger-led activities include discovery walks and bird watching. Families, schools and individuals can be involved with tree adoption and planting schemes.

Atherstone (near), Twycross Zoo, off A444, www.twycrosszoo.com 01827 880250. Set in 50 acres of parkland, the zoo has over 1000 animals, most of them rare species. This is a centre for education, conservation and fun. The famous primate collection ranges from the very small Pygmy Marmosets, to the huge Western Lowland Gorillas. See 'our closest living relative' - the Bonobo. Look out for the spider monkeys and young orang-utans. Other animals include elephants, lions, giraffe, pythons and crocodiles. If you like a good splash see the sealions, penguins and seals at feeding time (mid afternoon most days). During the Summer holidays at the 'Family Exhibition' in the Zoo Centre, experts will answer your animal questions. Visit the adventure playground before you leave, and in Summer take a ride on the miniature train. Various cafes, picnic areas and gift shops. Open daily, 10am-5.30pm (5pm in Winter). Schools **Open all year** Price C **Check out page 57.**

Desford, Tropical Birdland, Lindridge Lane, www.tropicalbirdland.co.uk 01455 824603. Set amongst five acres of woodland, there are birds from all over the world including toucans, parrots, macaws and emus. The baby bird viewing room is not to be missed. Open daily, Mar-mid Oct, 10am-5pm. Schools Price B.

Leicester, Gorse Hill City Farm, Anstey Lane, www.gorsehillcityfarm.co.uk 0116 253 7582. A registered charity with various animals and a new indoor education centre. Holiday workshops and a chance to become a volunteer worker. Open daily, 10am-4pm. Schools Birthdays **Open all year** Price A.

Moira, Conkers, Rawdon Road, www.visitconkers.com 01283 216633. Find out about The National Forest with a mix of indoor interactive exhibits and outdoor activities including a challenging assault course, woodland trails and a narrow-gauge railway train. Excellent play areas. Special events. Open daily, 10am-6pm (5pm Winter). Schools Birthdays **Open all year** Price B.

Mountsorrel, Stonehurst Family Farm, www.farm18.fsnet.co.uk 01509 413216. An award-winning farm with various animals and good playground. Explore the fields following a nature trail or enjoy a tractor and trailer ride. Tearoom, museum of vintage cars and special events. Open daily, 9.30am-5pm. Schools Birthdays **Open all year** Price B.

Tilton-on-the-Hill, Halstead House Farm, 0116 259 7239. In beautiful countryside see various farm animals and enjoy the field trail. Tractor and trailer rides, fishing lake, play and picnic areas. Open Easter-Sept, Tues-Sun and Bank Hol Mons, 10am-5.30pm. Schools Price A.

LINCOLNSHIRE

Alford (near), Claythorpe Watermill and Wildfowl Garden, www.claythorpewatermill.co.uk 01507 450687. This is a delightful place hidden in a wooded dell. See different birds and spot trout in the mill pools. Fairytale picnic and play area. Tearoom. Open daily, Mar-Oct, 10am-5pm (4pm early and late season). Plus special Christmas opening. Schools Price A.

Cleethorpes, Humber Estuary Discovery Centre, Lakeside, Kings Road, www.time-discoverycentre.co.uk 01472 323232. Enjoy a hands-on seaside exhibition. Try out the Punch and Judy puppets, use the telescopes and feed birds on the lake. Can you find the Meridian line? Open daily, 10am-5pm. Schools Birthdays **Open all year** Price A.

The Jungle, Lakeside, Kings Road, 01472 291998. Visit this mini-zoo to enjoy the wonderful sights and sounds of a tropical experience. See exotic plants, colourful parrots, toucans and reptiles. Open daily from 10am, closing times vary. Schools **Open all year** Price A.

Ingoldmells, Hardy's Animal Farm, Anchor Lane, 01754 872267. Adjacent to the beach caravans, an authentic rural smell greets you at this delightful farm park set in seven acres. Lots of animals to see, playground, horse and cart rides. Open daily, Easter-Oct, 10am-5pm. Schools Birthdays Price B.

Long Sutton, Butterfly and Wildlife Park, www.butterflyandwildlifepark.co.uk 01406 363833. An award-winning centre. Marvel at the wonderful butterflies and birds as you walk through a large tropical glasshouse. See crocodiles, a falconry display, wallabies and miniature ponies. Good adventure playground and crazy golf. Open daily, Mar-Oct, 10am-5pm. Schools Birthdays Price B.

Louth (near), Rushmoor Country Park, North Cockerington, signposted off B1200, www.rushmoorcountrypark.co.uk 01507 327184, is ideal for younger children. Relax in open countryside and see rare breed poultry. There are also small animals, a tearoom, picnic and play areas, and BBQ. Open daily, Easter-Oct, 10am-6pm. Schools Birthdays Price A.

Mablethorpe, Mablethorpe Seal Sanctuary, North End, 01507 473346, is set within the sand dunes. Some of the rescued seals from here are returned to the wild. Also, rescued seabirds and a wildcat breeding project. Open daily, Easter–end Sept, 10am-5pm. Sometimes open during Oct, phone for details. Schools Price B.

Newball, Woodside Falconry and Conservation Centre, signposted from A158, www.woodsidefalconry.co.uk 01522 754280. Watch a falconry display, have a go at fishing (all equipment supplied) or follow the woodland trail. The centre is set in beautiful surroundings. Open daily, 10am-5.30pm (4pm in Winter). Schools Birthdays **Open all year** Price B.

Skegness, Natureland Seal Sanctuary, North Parade, www.skegnessnatureland.co.uk 01754 764345. See the seals and penguins, an aquarium, tropical house with crocodiles and tarantulas, pets corner, butterflies and flamingos. Have a go at an animal brass rubbing and don't miss feeding time. Open daily, 10am–5pm (4pm Winter). Schools **Open all year** Price B.

Spalding (near), Baytree Owl Centre, Weston, signposted off the A16 bypass, 01406 372840. Part of a large garden nursery, the Owl Centre has over 70 birds and an indoor flying arena. Phone for details of flying demonstrations. Schools **Open all year** Price A.

Spilsby (near), Northcote Heavy Horse Centre, Great Steeping, www.northcote-horses.co.uk 01754 830286. A basic, no-frills centre where volunteers encourage children to help look after the horses. Stay all day and get involved. Horse and cart rides. Phone for opening times. Price B.

Wragby (near), Rand Farm Park, www.randfarmpark.com 01673 858904. Enjoy lots of animals and perhaps bottle-feed lambs, handle baby chickens or stroke the horses. Also tractor and trailer rides, play area, go-karts, sandpit and tearoom. Open daily, 10am-6pm (4pm Winter). Schools Birthdays **Open all year** Price B.

NOTTINGHAMSHIRE

Blyth, Hodsock Priory Garden, www.snowdrops.co.uk 01909 591204. Enjoy five acres of a beautiful woodland garden with a mass of snowdrops and other early Spring flowers. Open daily, end Jan-Mar, 10am-4pm. Price A.

East Leake, Manor Farm, Castle Hill, www.manorfarm.info 01509 852525. An award-winning animal centre and donkey sanctuary with over 200 animals. There is a picnic area, straw maze and cafe. Open Sat-Sun and Bank Hol Mons, 10am-5pm (4pm Winter), plus Tues-Fri during school hols, 10am-4pm. Birthdays **Open all year** Price B.

Edwinstowe (near), Sherwood Forest Farm Park, 01623 823558. A compact centre with various animals in paddocks, waterfowl and a pets corner with rabbits and goats. Open daily, 3rd Apr-17th Oct, 10.30am-5.15pm. Schools Birthdays Price B.

Farnsfield, White Post Farm Centre, www.whitepostfarmcentre.co.uk 01623 882977. Young children will really enjoy this busy place where there is lots to see and daily events that include feeding and handling some of the animals. Walk around the paddocks to see many different farm animals, while smaller animals can be found in various barns. There is even a reptile house with some impressive snakes! Enjoy the indoor playcentre and there are more playground areas outside, straw bales for climbing and pony rides. Open Mon-Fri, 10am-5pm. Schools Birthdays **Open all year** Price C **Check out page 57.**
Wonderland Pleasure Park, 01623 882773. Experience free-flying butterflies and birds in a giant tropical glasshouse. **Check out 'Adventure' chapter and inside back cover.**

Hoveringham, Ferry Farm, Boat Lane, www.ferryfarm.co.uk 0115 966 4512, is in an attractive position alongside the River Trent. See various rare breeds including Arnie, the largest

Italian ox in Britain. Pets corner, mini go-karts, an aerial zipline, ride-on tractors and tearoom. Open Easter-Sept, Tues-Sun and Bank Hol Mons, Oct, Sat-Sun and half term hol, 10am-5.30pm. Schools Birthdays Price B.

Normanton, Swan and Waterfowl Sanctuary, Reg Taylors Garden Centre, 01636 813184. Conservation area with six lakes. Buy bird food and see how many of the 60 species you can spot! Picnic areas. Open Mon-Sat, 10am-5.30pm, Sun, 10.30am-4.30pm. **Open all year** Price A.

RUTLAND

Egleton, Bird Watching Centre, 01572 770651. Internationally famous with a visitors centre and 22 hides along the shores of Rutland Water. Annual bird-watching festival weekend. Open daily, 9am-5pm (4pm Winter). Schools **Open all year** Price B.

Watch Badgers, 01572 770651. A pre-booked evening (in groups of six) starts with introductory slides and is followed by a visit to the hide. Children are welcome but must be very quiet. Available Apr-Aug, depending on a variety of circumstances.

Empingham (near), Butterfly & Aquatic Centre, Rutland Water, 01780 460515. Wander through the tropical greenhouse and admire the free-flying, colourful butterflies. See insects of all shapes and sizes and admire a superb display of local coarse and game fish. Open daily, end Mar-Oct, 10.30am-5pm (4.30pm Sept-Oct). Schools Price B.

Lyndon Hill, Visitor Centre and Nature Reserve, 01572 737378. Nature trails through woodland on the south shore of Rutland Water with six bird hides and good displays in the Visitor Centre. Open May-Oct, Tues-Thurs and Sat-Sun, Nov-Apr, Sat-Sun only, 10am-4pm. Schools **Open all year** Price A.

Places to go outside the area

Visit some exciting places just a little further afield.

BERKSHIRE

Windsor, LEGOLAND® www.legoland.co.uk 08705 040404, set in 150 acres of lovely parkland, offers an exciting and imaginative day out with lots of hands-on, interactive discovery. A brand new Jungle Coaster ride for 2004 promises thrills of acceleration, speed and high drops along a wild roller-coaster track that is themed to simulate an automobile test! Exciting experiences await as you wander through the Creation Centre, discover the Imagination Centre, enter LEGO® EXPLORE Land and have a go in the Driving School. Take the younger children to the Waterworks area, watch the daring stunt shows, scale the challenging Climbing Wall, brave the Pirate Falls and explore Miniland, made from over 35 million LEGO® bricks. Open 20th Mar-31st Oct, daily (except some Tues, Wed in Spring & Autumn), from 10am, closing times vary. Schools **Price G Check out page 58.**

STAFFORDSHIRE

Tamworth, SnowDome, LeisureIsland, River Drive, www.snowdome.co.uk 08705 000011, provides a wonderful opportunity to enjoy real snow! All members of the family can have great fun tobogganing, sledging, skiing, snowboarding, snow tubing and now you can ice skate too. Imagine racing your family and friends down the 170m snow slope in steerable toboggans, speeding down in specially designed inflatable tubes or just whizzing around the new ice rink! Tubing is available for 3-7s, 7-12s and over 12s. Younger children can also enjoy sledging sessions in the Snow Academy on special lightweight sledges. Pre-booking is advisable. Open daily, 9am-11pm, please telephone for slope timetable. Open all year Price E **Check out page 46.**

SUSSEX

Cambridge Language & Activity Courses. CLAC, www.clac.org.uk 01223 240340, organises interesting Summer courses for 8-13 year and 14-17 year olds at two separate sites in lovely countryside locations, Lavant House and Slindon College, West Sussex. The idea is to bring together British and foreign students to create natural language exchange in a motivated and fun environment. There are French, German and Spanish classes for British students and English for overseas students. Fully supervised in a safe environment, there are lots of activities such as swimming, tennis, team games and competitions, drama and music, in addition to the language tuition. Residential or not, these courses offer enjoyable multi-activity weeks with 20 hours of specific tuition in small groups. Courses run weekly during July and August. Please call for more details and a brochure. Birthdays **Check out page 68.**

Each choose a colour. Count how many vehicles of your chosen colour you see in a given time. Or the first one to reach ten.

Variations - This can also be played by choosing a number. Score 1 point for each number seen on a plate. If the number is repeated once on the same plate score 5 points and if 3 occur score 10 points. Either play with a time limit or the first to reach 20.

London

LET'S VISIT LONDON

BBC Television Centre Tours, Wood Lane, Shepherd's Bush, www.bbc.co.uk/tours 0870 6030304. Discover the history, the here and now as well as the digital future, of the most famous TV Centre in the world. Thousands of programmes are produced here every year including favourites such as Top of the Pops, Blue Peter, Parkinson and CBBC. On your tour you are likely to see into studios, visit BBC News, enter into the Top of the Pops Star Bar, play within the interactive studio and much more. Tours run 6 times a day, Mon-Sat and last for up to two hours. Tours are available for anyone over the age of 9 yrs and must be pre-booked. Television Centre is a working building so studio activity on the day of your visit cannot be guaranteed. The nearest Tube Station is White City on the Central Line. Schools **Open all year** Price C.

The London Aquarium, County Hall, Westminster Bridge Road, www.londonaquarium.co.uk 0207 967 8000 (information) 020 7967 8007 (school bookings). One of Europe's largest displays of aquatic life with over 350 species in over 50 displays, including the huge Pacific and Atlantic tanks. Information on the exciting daily feeds and talks can be found on the activities screen on arrival. Includes the spectacular Atlantic dive, where divers hand feed six foot long conger eels, rays and sharks. Educational tours and literature are available. Open daily, 10am-6pm (extended to 7pm in main holiday periods). Close to Westminster tube and Waterloo tube/mainline stations. Schools Birthdays **Open all year** Price C **Check out page 65.**

London's Transport Museum, Covent Garden Piazza, www.ltmuseum.co.uk 020 7565 7299 (recorded information), 020 7379 6344 (education service), using imaginative and dynamic displays, takes you on a fascinating journey through time and recounts the story of the interaction between transport, the capital and its people from 1800 to the present day. Look out for the under 5s funbus, try the bus and tube simulators, meet characters from the past, see models and working displays and get interactive in the many 'KidZones'. More fun learning than you would have thought possible! Good educational material and lots of special holiday activities. There is now free admission for children under 16. Open daily, 10am-6pm, but 11am-6pm on Fridays. Schools **Open all year** Price B **Check out page 60.**

LET'S TAKE A TRIP

On the River Thames with City Cruises, www.citycruises.com 02077 400 400. Add excitement for the children, a new perspective for everyone and get excellent value by seeing some of London's best sights from the River Thames aboard a City Cruises luxury river-liner using a River Red Rover ticket! You can travel as far as Greenwich to see the Cutty Sark. For just £8.70 for an adult ticket, £4.35 for a child or just £23 for a family ticket, you can use a hop-on hop-off service between the major destination piers on the River! From Westminster Pier services run every 20 minutes to Tower Pier, and, every 40 minutes to Greenwich via Waterloo and Tower Pier. Your River Red Rover will give you unlimited daily travel between these piers. Admire the Houses of Parliament, Big Ben and the London Eye, see St Paul's Cathedral and look out for the Tate Modern. Lots to see from these super boats with cafe style facilities and a capacity of 520 seats. **Open all year** Price C **Check out page 60.**

The Original Tour, London Sightseeing Bus Tours, www.theoriginaltour.com 020 8877 2120, provides a great way to introduce children to the splendid sights of London. The open top buses afford clear uncluttered views from a comfortable seat. You can hop-on and off at over 90 easily accessed stops. Children are both entertained and educated by the special commentary designed for them, as magical stories about London unfold with tales from Roman times until the present day. Listen out for the ghostly 'Spirit of London'. There is an exclusive 'Kids Club' too. The service runs frequently, seven days a week. Times vary seasonally for each route. Every customer is eligible for a free Thames River Cruise! For more information or to enjoy a special discount call 020 8877 2120 or visit www.theoriginaltour.com and quote LGWC. **Open all year** Price G **Check out page 60.**

Rainforest Cafe

A WILD PLACE TO SHOP AND EAT ®

**Combine animated wildlife and special effects.
Add phenomenal food made from the freshest ingredients and you've captured the breathtaking, dynamic features that embody Rainforest Cafe.**

FREE
SMOOTHIE OR DESSERT

With every main course ordered by your party

020 7434 3111

20 Shaftesbury Avenue, Piccadilly Circus, London W1D 7EU
www.therainforestcafe.co.uk

Please present to your safari guide when seated.
Cannot be used in conjunction with any other offer.

LET'S PLAY

Snakes and Ladders, Syon Park, Brentford, www.snakes-and-ladders.co.uk 020 8847 0946, is well signposted from Syon Park or can be accessed via 237 or 267 bus from Kew Bridge BR or Gunnersbury Underground Station. Children will find action packed fun whatever the weather. They can let off steam in the giant supervised indoor main play frame, intermediate 2-5s area or toddlers area and use the outdoor adventure playground when the sun shines. A mini motor-bike circuit provides an exciting additional activity, while parents can relax in the cafe overlooking the play frame. Open daily, 10am-6pm. All children must wear socks. Schools Birthdays **Open all year** Price A.

LET'S GO TO A CAFÉ

The Clay Café, 8-10 Monkville Parade, Finchley Road, Temple Fortune, www.theclaycafe.co.uk 020 8905 5353, is an exciting blend of cuisine and entertainment that positively welcomes families with children of all ages. The combination of a full service bistro style restaurant plus a paint-it-yourself ceramic studio offers a fresh and innovative approach to providing creative relaxation for both adults and children alike. Choose from over 200 pieces of pottery (dinnerware, vases, animals etc) and a qualified Art Technician will assist you in creating a unique masterpiece! Glass painting and T-shirt painting are also on offer. Open daily, Mon-Fri, 11am-10pm, Sat, 10am-11pm, Sun, 11am-10pm. Schools Birthdays **Open all year** Prices vary.

The Rainforest Cafe, 20 Shaftesbury Avenue, Piccadilly Circus, www.therainforestcafe.co.uk 020 7434 3111, brings the sights and sounds of a tropical rainforest into a 340-seat restaurant spanning three floors. Foods have wonderfully exciting names and there are many special effects including tropical rain showers, thunder and lightning storms, cascading waterfalls, rainforest mists and the cacophany of wildlife noises! Look out for tropical fish, chattering gorillas, trumpeting elephants, slithering boa and life-sized crocodile! Reservations possible at certain times with the exception of weekends and school holidays. Open Mon-Fri from 12noon, weekends and holidays open from 11.30am. Schools Birthdays **Open all year** Price G **Check out page 62.**

LET'S GO TO THE THEATRE

The Lion King, Lyceum Theatre, Wellington Street, www.disney.co.uk/MusicalTheatre 0870 243 9000 (ticket hotline), 020 7845 0949 (group bookings). One of the most successful Disney films in history, stunningly recreated on stage, is a thrilling and original musical which brings a rich sense of Africa to the stage through a medley of exotic sights and sounds. The show opens in the well loved Disney setting of 'Pride Rock' where 'Simba' the new lion cub is presented to a magical parade of Safari animals. One cannot fail to appreciate the inspiration that allows the giraffes to strut, the birds to swoop and the gazelles to bound. This initial spectacle is breathtaking as the entire savannah comes to life. Wonder at the creativity of the set as the sun rises, savannah plains sway, cattle stampede, drought takes hold and starry skies give up their secrets. Huge variety is offered in the musical score ranging from pulsating African rhythms to contemporary rock. Tim Rice and Elton John's Oscar winning work is unforgettable. A show not to be missed. **Open all year** Price G **Check out page 64.**

The Miz Kids' Club, is an exciting drama experience for children to go behind the scenes of the brilliant musical, Les Misérables, and to enjoy a matinee performance of the show. This is a great opportunity for children to enter the world of theatre and discover the fascination of a big West End production. Back stage, children see the costumes and props, hear the story of Les Misérables, learn one of the famous songs, join in drama games and improvise a key scene. Older children look at the technical operation of the stage effects and focus on characterisation in their improvisation workshop. The clubs meet before the Saturday matinee at 10.30am for 8–11s and 10.45am for 12–15s, both finishing at 1.15pm. Packages, from £23, include a CD synopsis of Les Misérables, sent in advance of their visit, a snack packed lunch and a ticket to the performance on the day. For details visit www.lesmis.com or call 020 7439 3062. **Open all year Check out page 64.**

OCEANS OF COLOUR

From sharks, stingrays and
piranhas to moray eels,
lionfish and sideways walking
crabs, London Aquarium
is full of surprises with
350 different species
to discover.

Located in County Hall, right
next to the London Eye, the
London Aquarium is just over
Westminster Bridge from
Big Ben and the Houses of
Parliament, and a short walk
from Waterloo station.

So, don't plan a day out in
London without visiting
London's only Aquarium!

Check out our special group,
family and school rates.

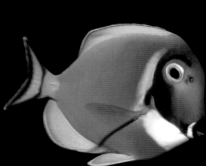

LONDON
AQUARIUM

FLOOD YOUR SENSES

Tel 020 7967 8000   www.londonaquarium.co.uk

Can't find a babysitter?

SitterS
0800 38 900 38

For Evening Babysitters
www.sitters.co.uk

Evening Babysitters with Professional Childcare Experience

Now you can find mature, friendly and reliable evening babysitters, available at short notice. For your reassurance we interview each babysitter in person and check all references thoroughly.

All Sitters babysitters have professional childcare experience and most are local authority registered childminders or professionally qualified nursery nurses.

How does Sitters' service work

When you make a booking we arrange for a babysitter to attend at the appointed time. At the end of the evening you pay the babysitter for the hours they have worked. Babysitting rates start from £4.40 per hour and vary depending on your area. There are no additional charges for travelling costs and all bookings are for a minimum of 4 hours.

Each time you book a babysitter we charge a nominal £4 booking fee to your credit card. You can register with Sitters free! Membership of just £12.75 for 3 months will only be charged <u>after</u> your first sitting. Call us today - less than £1 per week is a small price to ensure your children are in experienced hands.

For more information, phone us FREE today or

0800 38 900 38
or visit us at www.sitters.co.uk
Please quote Ref: LET'S GO

Experienced Childcarers Needed

Sitters welcomes applications from suitable babysitters. You will need to be over 21, have professional childcare experience, your own transport and immaculate references. For more information and to register your interest phone 0800 38 900 38 or visit www.sitters.co.uk.

Recruitment & Employment Confederation

We're in  YELLOW PAGES

INVESTOR IN PE⬤

Index